"*Like having coffee with an expert*"

ALSO BY ROHIT BHARGAVA

Personality Not Included

Likeonomics

Always Eat Left-Handed

Non-Obvious Megatrends

The Non-Obvious Guide to
Marketing & Branding

WORKING REMOTELY

Being Productive Without Getting Distracted, Lonely, or Bored

IDEAPRESS
PUBLISHING

BY ROHIT BHARGAVA

IDEAPRESS
PUBLISHING

Published in the United States by Ideapress Publishing.
All trademarks are the property of their respective companies.
Cover Design by Victoria Kim
Cataloging-in-Publication Data is on file with the Library of Congress.
ISBN: 978-1-64687-044-8

Special Sales
Ideapress Books are available at a special discount for bulk
purchases for sales promotions and premiums, or for use
in corporate training programs. Special editions, including
personalized covers, a custom foreword, corporate imprints, and
bonus content are also available.

Non-Obvious® is a registered trademark of the Influential
Marketing Group.

Read this book to learn how to avoid distractions and be more productive when doing remote work. Whether you need to collaborate with people virtually, deliver a compelling virtual presentation, or lead a remote team, this book will give you step-by-step advice on how to do it.

Is This Guide for You?

As the publisher of this series, I have the privilege of writing introductory notes for every one of these **Non-Obvious Guides.** Usually, I rave about our amazing authors and why they are so brilliantly qualified to write their respective guides.

For this guide, I happen to also be the author ... and I'm sure you wouldn't want to hear me rave about myself. So instead, I will tell you that this book was written in response to the COVID-19 pandemic - but it's meant to be used far beyond this moment of distanced work.

Learning to work remotely is not only a current necessity, but also a skill most of us will need in the years to come. The hybrid future of work will be in the office and remote. We all need to be ready for it.

ROHIT BHARGAVA
Founder, Non-Obvious Guides

CONTENTS

How to Read This Book

Throughout this book, you will find links to helpful guides and resources online.

FOR ONLINE RESOURCES, VISIT:

www.nonobviousguides.com/remotework

Referenced in the book, you will also see these symbols which refer to content that will further your learning.

— FOLLOW THE ICONS: —

TEMPLATES
One-page templates to help explain concepts.

DOWNLOADS
Excerpts or useful further reading.

TUTORIALS
Detailed lessons on how to do a task.

VIDEOS
Videos to watch online.

CHAPTER SUMMARY
Key takeaways and important points.

In this book, you will learn how to . . .

- ✔ Avoid distractions and be more productive no matter what happens around you.

- ✔ Choose the right technology to get things done more quickly and easily.

- ✔ Assess your working style to divide your day between deep vs. shallow work.

- ✔ Effectively lead a virtual team and improve accountability.

- ✔ Conquer the loneliness and isolation that often comes with remote work.

- ✔ Deliver a compelling virtual presentation in a meeting, webinar, or online training session.

- ✔ Collaborate with people you've never met and colleagues working remotely.

- ✔ Manage and prevent conflicts in a virtual setting with increased emotional intelligence.

Introduction

It was the winter of 2004, and the large marketing agency where I worked had just moved into a new office in downtown Washington, D.C.

As part of the move, our seating chart was being completely changed. The day the assignments came out, we all rushed to read the list as if we were high schoolers checking the cast list for the winter musical.

It was a good day. I had been given an office with a window. In the new building, those were prized possessions, so earning one of my own was a big deal.

> It was the first time in my life that I ever had an office. It also would be the last.

For the next several years, that office became like a second home. Colleagues would come by to have impromptu brainstorming sessions, post-work drinks, and therapeutic venting sessions after a difficult client call.

The office was where our team bonding happened.

A few years later, my wife and I were expecting our second baby, and I had just been offered a publishing deal to write my first book, *Personality Not Included*.

To manage the workload, I went to my boss and made the unusual request to have every Friday off for five months to write the book. He agreed.

During that time, I had been assigned to a team that worked nationally, so I was spending one day a week working from our Manhattan office, in addition to writing from home on Fridays. A few weeks before my book deadline, I received a brief email from the head of our D.C. office.

It was a short note informing me that since I was never in my office, it was being reassigned to someone who would use it more regularly. I was devastated and angry.

That was my office, the one I had worked hard to earn. This wasn't fair. I immediately felt the urge to fight to keep it until my wife logically explained that if I did that, I would probably have to go into the office more often to justify why I needed it.

That night, as I held my three-week-old son in one arm and typed with the other, I knew I didn't want to go into the office anymore.

Working on the final chapters for my book (with Jaiden's help)!

I was lucky enough to have a job with so much flexibility that I didn't have to choose between bonding with my son and commuting to the office every day, and despite my one travel day to New York every week, I was still getting to be home much more.

So, I continued along my remote working journey, vowing never to look back.

Until I started feeling something was wrong.

I started to *miss* going into the office.

See the glossary for definitions of highlighted terms. ➤

It had been three years since I had chosen the life of a **digital nomad** working inside a large company. I had no office space, used **hot desks** when I went into any of our offices around the world, and had no office location printed on my business cards.

Over that time, business had gone well, and our agency had landed some huge new clients. The book had done well and my reputation as an engaging keynote speaker was also growing. I was starting to get paid invitations to deliver talks at conferences around the world.

But I no longer had the close connection with my colleagues I once enjoyed.

Every time I visited the office, I saw new team members I didn't recognize ... and they didn't know me either. What made it even harder to accept was the fact that I had chosen this working lifestyle.

In just a few years, I had gone from a remote working enthusiast to a lonely and disconnected virtual team member.

Wait, I hear you thinking ... isn't this supposed to be a book about how awesome it is to work remotely and how great virtual meetings can be? Actually, no, it isn't.

> Working remotely isn't better than being face to face. But sometimes you don't have a choice.

My aim with this book is not to persuade you that working remotely is better than any other arrangement.

As much as we want to tell ourselves that we can do virtual meetings and be more productive without the distractions of colleagues, the serendipity that happens when you are with co-workers is hard to recreate virtually.

In a great work environment, the people around you will challenge and inspire you to be better.

WHY YOU SHOULD READ THIS BOOK

The goal of this book isn't to pretend that working remotely is always better or that offices are irrelevant. Instead, you will read about how you can continue to make human connections, collaborate effectively, present virtually, and do business without being in the same room.

It's a book for a world forever changed by a global pandemic, where more employers might ask you to stay home, avoid the office, skip the commute, and be productive from afar.

The future of business is going to require this sort of flexibility. In this book, you'll find a collection of the skills, habits, and techniques to help you get ready for the new reality of modern work.

PART ONE

Working Remotely

CHAPTER 1

Remote Work 101

The founders of Basecamp, a popular project management platform, described the modern office as an "interruption factory," observing that "a busy office is like a food processor – it chops your day into tiny bits."[1]

In the popular television show *The Office*, the "modern workplace" is portrayed as an outdated ritual, filled with time-wasting colleagues and meaningless meetings.

The traditional office, once seen as a standard part of our working life, is becoming increasingly optional. Instead, more people are opting to work from places other than the office. And since the pandemic, they have had no other choice.

The option and opportunity to work remotely has gone from an indulgence and hallmark of the freelance lifestyle to a daily necessity for the majority of office workers.

1.1	**Three Factors Leading to a Rise in Remote Work**

According to one survey, more than half of the world's employees work from home at least once per week, and 18 percent of people work remotely full-time.[2]

Given these numbers, it would be easy to think that remote work is a recent trend. After all, the types of jobs we often hear people doing remotely seem to be modern expertises, such as web designers or virtual assistants. For most of human history, though, working remotely was actually the norm.

Remote work is hundreds of years old.

In medieval times, most artisans worked from home. The famous tenements of the early 1900s in New York were examples of people working from home. Even the term **telecommuting** is more than 50 years old, originally coined by NASA engineer Jack Nilles in 1972.[3]

Building on remote work's long history, three factors are accelerating the ability of people to work from anywhere:

1. **Ease of communication:** Thanks to our advanced communications tools and the Internet, it has become easier to communicate in real time and collaborate without being there in person.

2. **Rise of information work:** As we live in a time where information has become a commodity, the nature of our work has shifted. More people work with information and content today than ever before.

3. **Disruption of work:** The COVID-19 pandemic has clearly forced a change in the number of people working remotely. Even before coronavirus, developments in globalization and dispersal of teams have contributed to the rise of remote work.

The bottom line is that more work is getting done outside the traditional confines of the office, and this trend shows no signs of slowing.

1.2	**Why People Love Remote Work**

If you do a quick search for online advice about working remotely or browse any bookstore for written advice on the topic, you'll generally find a single point of view: Remote work is better.

Most of the time, it is because of three reasons:

1. MORE FLEXIBILITY

This is a huge factor, particularly among the younger generation. One study found that 69 percent of millennials would give up other work benefits for a more flexible working space, and another found that companies that allowed remote work had 25 percent lower employee turnover.[4] The bottom line is, the more control people have over where they do their work, the happier and more loyal they will be.

2. FEWER DISTRACTIONS

Anyone who has worked in offices knows that they indeed can be distraction factories, laden with unexpected drop-ins, unnecessary meetings, and time-filling tedium that doesn't accomplish anything. When you're working remotely, many of these distractions disappear. Unfortunately, as you'll read in later sections of this book, they are often replaced by other types of distractions.

3. BETTER LIFESTYLE

One disturbing Swedish study found that couples with commutes of 45 minutes or longer had a 40 percent greater risk of divorce.[5] While this may seem like an extreme statistic, those who love remote work often talk about their ability to live in a beloved place, commute-free, as an important benefit of leaving the office life behind.

1.3   Why Companies Love Remote Workers

Though remote work is often described as a benefit offered to employees by reluctant companies, the truth is that there are several reasons why companies might prefer for employees to work remotely:

1. **Lower Cost:** Research published by Global Workforce Analytics found that the average real estate savings per remote worker was $10,000. It noted that allowing this type of work helped IBM to save more than $50 million in real estate costs.[6] When combined with the lower costs for office supplies, support staff, workplace perks, and other routine expenses, the numbers really add up.

2. **More Productivity:** In a fascinating two-year study profiled in his TEDx Talk, Stanford Professor Nicholas Bloom shared the results on the benefits of working from home at one large Shanghai-based company. His research showed that a group of employees working from home had a huge productivity boost compared with their counterparts in the office.[7] Many other companies found similar results.

3. **Higher Loyalty:** The numbers also show that the more control you give to people around how they work, the more loyal they are.[8] This translates into lower turnover and better results in the long run.

1.4   The Difference Between Working Remotely and Working from Home

Working from home is usually a temporary choice, often made out of necessity or convenience. Remote work, on the other hand, is work done consistently and intentionally outside the traditional office.

When you're working from home, you might want to prioritize the tasks that are better done out of the office because you have precious uninterrupted time. If you work from home once per week, for example, you may want to avoid all meetings on that day since you can do those meetings in person anyway.

With remote work, it is more important to establish a more regular routine, particularly for a future that probably will include far more **hybrid work** than most of us do today. Hybrid work is the combination of working from an office and working remotely.

Either way, as Harvard Business School Professor Tsedal Neeley notes, "remote work is actually a learned skill. People don't just do it well organically. So it's important to help people, to coach people, to provide resources on how to do it well."[9]

1.5 Seven Challenges of Working Remotely

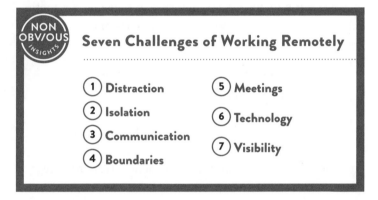

Seven Challenges of Working Remotely

(1) Distraction   (5) Meetings

(2) Isolation   (6) Technology

(3) Communication   (7) Visibility

(4) Boundaries

Fifty years ago, UCLA Professor Albert Mehrabian published a book called *Silent Messages,* in which he suggested that 93 percent of all communication is nonverbal.[10] If that's true, then working remotely poses some obvious challenges.

This isn't the only challenge of being a remote worker. The Internet is filled with discussion about the problems of working remotely. Let's take a candid look at some of the most common:

CHALLENGE 1 **DISTRACTION**

Whether you consider yourself someone who is easily distracted or not, the truth is that our homes or other places we might work from can be filled with distractions. Sometimes they are immediate (someone ringing the doorbell or a dog barking), and sometimes they are self-inflicted (the temptation to binge-watch another episode of your favorite show or to snack constantly).

> "The three great enemies of working from home are the fridge, the bed, and the TV."[11]

For more on how to conquer your distractions, turn to page 21.

CHALLENGE 2 **ISOLATION AND LONELINESS**

It is natural to crave human connection, and people new to working remotely often cite isolation and loneliness as their biggest struggle. The first thing to remember is that isolation and loneliness often can be two different problems.

Isolation is a feeling of disconnection that can come from processes or a workplace culture that removes them from colleagues or information. Loneliness, on the other hand, is an emotional state and can happen with those working remotely as well as those who go to an office.

Working without colleagues around can be lonely, and the sense of isolation can lead to depression or a feeling of disconnection from everyone else. Even if you have virtual meetings regularly or visit the office on occasion to meet with people, this is one of the most common and natural emotions you may feel.

For more on how to deal with the isolation, turn to page 26.

CHALLENGE 3 COMMUNICATION AND COLLABORATION

Most of us are not accustomed to collaborating with others effectively without doing so face to face, and unfortunately we never had much training on how to do it. Adding to the problem is the fact that there are so many ways to communicate today, from video conferencing to instant messaging to email. It's hard to know what to use and when to use it. The ironic truth is that we feel disconnected even though we have so many technologies to help us connect.

For tips to improve your communication, turn to page 119.

CHALLENGE 4 WORK-LIFE BOUNDARIES

One of the real dangers of working remotely is overworking. Since your day is no longer dictated by the traditional 9-to-5 schedule, you may find yourself working far more hours than if you were in the office. This is particularly true in the cases where you have a global team working across time zones, requiring you to work odd hours.

For more on how to set boundaries, turn to page 32.

PERSPECTIVE:
SHELLY PALMER ON OFFICE HOURS

If you are supposed to work from 9 to 5, then work 9 to 5. Take the same breaks you'd take if you were in the office, including – and this is important – lunch! Regular hours increase productivity. I promise.[12]

> – *Shelly Palmer is an advertising, marketing, and technology consultant and business adviser.*

CHALLENGE 5 MEETINGS

A virtual meeting is very different than an in-person one. Virtual meetings actually make it harder to collaborate, and most people lack the training to run them well. When they don't work, virtual meetings become a source of frustration for everyone involved.

For tips on running or participating in virtual meetings, turn to Part II, which features four chapters on the topic.

CHALLENGE 6 TECHNOLOGY

The same thing that enables many of us to work from home can be a barrier to doing it effectively. Sometimes the technology just doesn't work, or we don't have it set up correctly to allow us to work.

For more on how to set up technology to help you work better, turn to page 39.

CHALLENGE 7 **VISIBILITY**

This final challenge is the one I shared in my book introduction about feeling invisible within an organization and suffering for it. When you aren't there in person, you'll need to work doubly hard to make sure you aren't neglected, dismissed, or forgotten.

To learn how to promote yourself and ensure you don't become invisible, turn to page 47.

CHAPTER SUMMARY
KEY TAKEAWAYS:

- Remote work is not a recent phenomenon. People have been working remotely for hundreds of years.

- Contrary to what many leaders believe, studies show people who work remotely can often be more productive than those who commute to an office every day.

- There are seven big challenges of working remotely that need to be overcome: distraction, isolation, communication, boundaries, meetings, technology, and visibility.

Chapter 2

The Remote Working Lifestyle

Remember Professor Nicholas Bloom's research from the last chapter? There is one more conclusion from his studies that I didn't mention yet. At the end of his nine-month research program investigating the differences in productivity between groups of workers at a large Chinese company who were randomly assigned to work from home and or told to continue working from the office, the company decided to offer a choice to all employees.

Almost immediately, a significant number of the workers who had been assigned to work from home decided to switch back to coming into the office every day. At the same time, some but not all the workers who had been required to come into work every day chose the remote work option.

After the employees were allowed to choose, the overall productivity of the entire company rose even further. It turned out that people working from home weren't inherently more productive unless they wanted to work from home.

2.1 The Five Habits of Remote Workers Who Get More Done

Is it possible that some people are better suited to working remotely than others? You probably know some people who are better self-starters or show more introverted tendencies, and you might suppose that remote work would fit their personalities better.

During more than a decade of working with colleagues remotely and in person, I have realized this isn't true. Anyone can learn to be more productive when working remotely. Starting with these five habits will help.

NON OBVIOUS INSIGHTS

Five Habits of Remote Workers Who Get More Done

1. Set Brave Boundaries
2. Give Undivided Focus
3. Have Creative Resilience
4. Practice Virtual Empathy
5. Use Deliberate Clarity

HABIT 1 SET BRAVE BOUNDARIES

When your commute time is three minutes, it's always going to be tempting to go to work at any hour of the day. The flexibility is one of the great advantages of remote work. It can also be the biggest challenge. Your overall sanity depends on your ability to set the right boundaries between work and your life. This is particularly important when work and life are happening just a bedroom away from one another. In order to get more done, be brave about where you will create those boundaries, and stick to them.

For more advice on how to set brave boundaries, read Chapter 3.

HABIT 2 GIVE UNDIVIDED FOCUS

Distractions are a normal part of any working day, but you may find that they become far more tempting and unavoidable when you are working from home. There are always dishes to put away or a comfortable place to lie down for a moment. No matter whether you're working from home or remotely from another location, the ability to focus while remote is a critical skill you will need to learn and practice.

For advice on growing your ability to have undivided focus, read the later sections in this chapter.

HABIT 3 HAVE CREATIVE RESILIENCE

When working alone in a more open-ended environment, being able to think like a self-starter is critical. The people who adjust best to remote work train themselves to be more proactive, entrepreneurial, and motivated. The best remote workers are uncomfortable with the status quo. They avoid complacency and are not afraid to disrupt themselves when necessary. Most of all, they know that any work situation can change quickly – from where they work to the nature of their job. As a result, they learn to be more flexible and adaptable for the future.

For advice on how to be creatively resilient, read Chapter 11.

HABIT 4 PRACTICE VIRTUAL EMPATHY

Empathy is the ability to understand and appreciate what others are feeling. Doing it virtually requires a combination of creativity and observation.

> The people who understand people always win.

This is something I often say during my keynote presentations. The truth is that the more we can understand the mindsets of the people we deal with, the more persuasive and valuable we can be as a teammate, leader, or service provider.

For advice on practicing more virtual empathy, read Chapter 10.

HABIT 5 USE DELIBERATE CLARITY

It took me far too long to realize that the most effective way to communicate is to do the opposite of what I was expected to do in my Comparative Literature class back in university. In the class, I was expected to use the biggest words I could imagine and work hard to make every sentence a work of art. In business, most people hate that. Clarity is the ability to express yourself in a straightforward way that people easily understand.

For advice on how to use deliberate clarity with teammates, read Chapter 9.

2.2 How to Set an Efficient Schedule

How do you plan your day when you are working remotely? In some areas, such as prescheduled meetings, you may not have much choice about when you work. But here are some techniques to help you create an optimal schedule for the rest of the day.

TIP 1 CALENDAR WHAT YOU HATE

Most normal people push the things they hate doing to the bottom of their lists. It's the reason so many of us do our taxes right before the deadline. However, if you put the things you hate on your calendar earlier, it is more likely you will do them earlier too.

TIP 2 START YOUR DAY OFFLINE

You have the chance to set your mindset for the entire day based on what you choose to do first. So hide the phone (or charge it overnight somewhere other than right by your bed!). Instead, find a morning ritual that helps you get grounded and proactively ready for the day.

PERSPECTIVE:
AUSTIN KLEON ON MORNING RITUALS

There's almost nothing in the news that any of us need to read in the first hour of the day. When you reach for your phone or your laptop upon waking, you're immediately inviting anxiety and chaos into your life. You're also bidding adieu to some of the most potentially fertile moments in the life of a creative person.[13]

 — *Austin Kleon is a bestselling author of three books, including* Steal Like an Artist *and* Show Your Work!

TIP 3 KNOW YOUR DEAD TIMES

I can't write in the afternoon. From 3 p.m. to 6 p.m., I will stare at the screen and get nothing done. So several years ago I decided to stop trying. Now I'll often schedule phone calls in that time span, or coach soccer practice with my kids, or respond to email. The point is that those afternoon hours are now productive for me because I am intentional about what I choose not to do.

TIP 4 GROUP YOUR MEETINGS

Meetings are notorious for becoming interruptions that stand in the way of getting real work done. Why not group them back to back in a single part of your day? That not only can help you get them all done, but also can give you an excuse to make sure that each one ends on time. Then you can leave since you have another call to make.

PERSPECTIVE:
JOEL GASCOIGNE ON "THEME DAYS"

I generally theme my days. Some are focused on managing and supporting my awesome executive team. Other days, I'm working on the product, putting together documents for strategy and process improvement, or digging into customer research or product metrics to find opportunities.[14]

– *Joel Gascoigne is the founder of Buffer, a social media management platform.*

TIP 5 BLOCK TIME FOR WORK

I used to have a calendar so filled with meetings that I didn't have time for anything else. So I started blocking time for writing and other work. Technically I was blocking time for "work" because I didn't always know what I would be doing then. Having that time unavailable on my calendar became a big deal – especially after I started allowing other members of my team to add meetings to my calendar without approval in advance.

TIP 6 SET OFFICE HOURS

Setting specific hours when you will be working each day (and when you won't!) has many benefits. It can help to motivate yourself and tell your teammates when you're available. It also can let family or others who live with you know when you are not available. That can help minimize the number of times you are interrupted during the day.

PERSPECTIVE:
BRIAN FANZO ON WORKING WITH ADHD

I firmly believe there isn't just one right way of working from home. As someone with ADHD, I like to learn from multiple different people in multiple different formats. Many would guess working from home would create laziness but it's more likely to lead to burnout because working from home requires a new life mindset, not just a work location change![15]

– Brian Fanzo is a digital futurist and founder of iSocialFanz.

2.3 | How to Stay Focused and Avoid Distractions

Conquering the many distractions while working remotely is an ongoing battle and one that I often lose too. However, I do understand why I lose that battle. In this section, I'll share some techniques that have helped me to stay focused even when a seemingly constant stream of distractions is conspiring for my attention.

TIP 1 USE THE FIVE-SECOND RULE

My friend Mel Robbins has written about something she calls the Five-Second Rule: "If you have an instinct to act on a goal, you must physically move within five seconds, or your brain will kill it." Her advice to avoid this is simple. "When you feel yourself hesitate before doing something that you know you should do, count 5-4-3-2-1-GO and move toward action."[16]

It turns out this rule is surprisingly effective to help yourself avoid distractions as well. If you feel yourself getting off task, use Mel's rule to reset and focus yourself.

TIP 2 INTEGRATE WHITE NOISE

When I'm writing or trying to concentrate, I prefer having some ambient noise. It turns out I'm not alone. Most people concentrate better when there is white noise in the background. Also some sound can help to drown out the more distracting noises that you can't silence, such as boarding announcements or barking dogs.

My favorite tool for generating white noise on demand is an app and website called Coffitivity (www.coffitivity.com), which simulates the sounds of a coffee shop. I've written three books (including this one) while playing Coffitivity in the background.

PERSPECTIVE:
PAMELA SLIM ON TAKING A MENTAL BREAK

When you spend a good amount of time working remotely, your physical environment becomes increasingly important. Add multi-sensory elements to your space (a fountain, a candle, beautiful art on the wall, favorite books or objects, a polished stone).

When you take a break from your keyboard, turn to the burning candle and look into the flame. Close your eyes and listen to the ripple of the water from the fountain. Pick up the smooth stone on your desk and feel the weight and texture. Such actions shift your focus from your brain to the rest of your body and clear the fog of screen overload.[17]

- *Pamela Slim is the author of* Body of Work *and* Escape from Cubicle Nation.

TIP 3 ADD FRICTION

For many of us, social media is our most constant source of distraction. One of the reasons why it can be so distracting is that it's so easy to check your feed whenever your mind wanders. Here are a few tricks I use to minimize the potential diversion by social media:

→ Disable all alerts and notifications.

→ Remove the apps from your phone or organize them in sub-folders to make them harder to reach.

→ Set automatic logout timers so you are forced to log back in every time.

→ Download the "lite" and less functional versions of popular social media apps. These can be frustratingly slow and inelegant to use, which means you'll end up using them less because it is no longer fun.

→ Use tools that help manage your screen time by locking your apps when you reach your predefined limit.

→ Turn off the Internet. Yes, believe it or not, there is a feature on every computer that allows you to disable your WiFi and go offline – but you may never have used it!

→ If you have a home office, add a note for delivery services instructing them NOT to ring the doorbell and just to leave packages outside so you're not disturbed while working.

→ Post less often! The less you post, the less temptation you have to constantly check who engaged with your content.

TIP 4 TIME SHIFT YOUR DAY

In his book *When*, author Dan Pink argues that if we want to optimize our productivity, we should move our most important and concentration-heavy tasks to the morning when our ability to concentrate is higher.

The ideal way to start your day is *not* by checking email or spending time on social media.

Instead, try to spend the first part of your morning planning what you want to accomplish that day instead of reacting to the latest "urgent" email.

Attention expert and speaker Neen James suggests to also "invest 15 minutes in a strategic appointment with yourself every day; identify your top 3 not-negotiable activities, write them on a post-it note and use this as your daily decision filtering system."[18]

TIP 5 BE LESS AVAILABLE

It's tempting to respond to texts, emails, and social media comments right away. The problem when you do that is that you're building an expectation from your friends, family, and colleagues that you'll always respond instantly, setting yourself up for distractions. Instead, set automated replies for social media, use "away from my desk" settings, and funnel people toward the best way to reach you.

For example, I don't use Facebook messenger to connect. Anytime I get a message from my page, this is what people see as a response:

"Thanks for the message. This is an automated reply to say this isn't the best way to get in touch with me. Please use the form on www.rohitbhargava.com or send me an email instead to connect."

2.4 How to Conquer Isolation and Loneliness

There are some smart ways that you can address both issues, feel more connected with work, keep your sanity, and connect with others while working remotely.

1. AUDIT THE ISOLATION MOMENTS

Back when I was working in that office in D.C., I used to get interoffice emails about colleagues' birthday parties. Then one day they stopped. Modern workplaces are full of moments like this when remote workers are unintentionally cut off from the team, but we can prevent that if we can understand when they happen.

Back then, I never mentioned to anyone how it made me feel to be taken off the list, and no one ever asked. Looking back now, I use the example as a reminder for myself and leaders whom I advise that you need to be more aware of these small things in order to identify them ... and then you can do something to fix them.

2. CONNECT WITH INDIVIDUALS

Spending too much time on social media seeing how connected everyone else seems is a recipe for making yourself lonelier. Instead, reach out to reconnect with people individually. You might be surprised how many friends who appear to have amazingly complete lives on social media are just as hungry for a real connection as you are.

PERSPECTIVE:
TODD CAPONI ON GETTING SUPPORT

Find at least one person (not a family member) with whom you can talk to – about personal worries, issues, potential decisions, and feelings. Once you do, seek ways to make sure that's happening in your teams. Do your team members have an individual outside work they can confide in?

This doesn't have to be a "mentor." It's OK to just have someone who's at any level. Just make sure you find someone.[19]

–*Todd Caponi is a sales leader and the author of*
The Transparency Sale.

3. FOCUS ON GIVING AND SHARING

When you focus on what you can give instead of what you miss, you can change your perspective. Could you find a volunteer group where your expertise or time might be valued? Not only can this be of great value for your community, but also you can feel positive yourself and make some connections in the process.

4. ACCEPT MORE INVITATIONS

Anytime I started to feel disconnected from colleagues, I realized it was at least partially self-inflicted. I was too busy to go to the events I had been invited to (real or virtual). Don't make the same mistake. When you are invited to participate, make it happen.

5. FIND A MENTOR (OR BECOME ONE)

Many modern companies are using programs such as **reverse mentors** to ensure everyone feels connected – even those working remotely. If your company has a program like that, join it. If not, try to find a similar group in your area that runs this type of program.

6. SPEND MONEY ON AN EXPERIENCE

Any number of self-help books will tell you that the path to happiness lies in focusing on experiences instead of accumulating more stuff. Think about how you might spend money on an experience that can allow you to feel more connected with other people and challenge yourself to do something new and unusual, whether it is jumping out of a plane or trying new cuisine.

2.5 Five Mindfulness Principles to Make Remote Work Better

Contributed by Paresh and Eliza Shah, founders of Lifter Leadership.

Some people associate mindfulness and yoga with sweaty spandex-clad people who greet their day with downward dog and sit like pretzels. But mindfulness and yoga are much more than a physical fitness practice.

As millions of people (from top business performers to athletes, creative artists, students, and entrepreneurs) are realizing, the ancient practices of mindfulness deliver a range of powerful benefits, from less stress to laser-caliber focus, hearing customer needs better, innovating brilliant solutions, elevating difficult conversations, and ultimately, getting more of the right stuff done with less time and effort.

A great benefit of mindfulness that many remote workers are taking advantage of is the ability to intersperse short mindful practices between meetings, to boost performance, without concern of seeming odd or disrupting co-workers.

It's an invisible competitive advantage that is counter-intuitive to our busy "must do more" mindset. As practitioners and trainers of mindful leadership, every day we witness the evidence of what at first seemed silly to us when we heard it.

Mahatma Gandhi once said, "I have so much to accomplish today that I must meditate for two hours instead of one."

We are not advocating that you need to spend anywhere near an hour to boost your work performance dramatically to tap into the practical business, career, relationship, and health benefits of non-obvious mindfulness in action.

Here are some mindful tips and practices to help you get more done while working remotely.

TIP 1 HAVE A STRAIGHT SPINE

A simple practice to boost your remote productivity is to simply focus on your posture and sit (or stand) straight to activate your best thinking. Like trying to water your garden with a kinked hose, sitting with a bent spine can slow down or even block neural connections you need to activate the awesome within you.

TIP 2 HAVE MINI-GRATITUDE CELEBRATIONS

When switching between tasks, meetings, and family time, have a mini-celebration signaling completion to your mind and body – this could be washing your hands with a smile, playing fetch with your dog, picking up your guitar, or making that lovably imperfect video sharable online. Mini-celebrations are like a palette cleanser and signal the start of a new time-space.

TIP 3 SINGLE NOSTRIL BREATHING

For more energy or calming, work with your parasympathetic nervous system by breathing as follows: For more energy, if bored or sleepy, breathe strongly through your right nostril (your sun center, according to yoga). To calm, cool, or relax yourself under stress, breathe through your left nostril (your moon center).

TIP 4 USE A "ONE WORD" OPEN AND CLOSE

When clients ask us to facilitate their virtual meetings and workshops, we kick them off and end with each team member sharing one word to express how they feel. We do not go into any explanations. This approach presents a golden opportunity to feel empathy for teammates, acknowledges where people are, and engages mindful listening at the start and end of meetings.

TIP 5 TALK LESS, SMILE MORE

Sometimes, remote workers feel job insecurity and speak more, hoping the boss will notice them. Instead, allow what you feel you want to share to "mature" through three waves of the urge to speak. Trust that the moment for your contribution to land will arrive. Your contribution will be powerful. By actively listening and being highly present, even in silence, you become visible. Presence is the new visibility.

Paresh and Eliza Mountcastle Shah, PhD, are founders of Lifter Leadership, a global training and development firm.

2.6   Three Ways to Create Remote Work-Life Balance

When working remotely, it is far too easy to let work take over all parts of your day. How do you create a better balance between your work and real life? Here are some proven techniques that may help:

1. Create daily rituals to help separate your day and set moments when you know it's time to stop working. For example, block time for a class or set a quitting time for yourself – and then follow it.

2. Go offline and turn off your devices to allow yourself to think and to offer a separation from your work. When you do this in the morning, you can help set yourself up for a productive day getting your work and your personal goals both done.

3. If you work late or on the weekend, schedule messages to send automatically during business hours so people don't expect you to be available on email at all hours because they see you sending emails late.*

Note: The exception to this rule is when you want your boss or colleagues to know that you're working late – but during those moments, you're probably not prioritizing a work-life balance anyway.

CHAPTER SUMMARY
KEY TAKEAWAYS:

- There are five habits of remote workers who get more done: they set brave boundaries, know how to be creatively resilient, have undivided focus when it matters, practice virtual empathy, and use deliberate clarity.

- To set an efficient schedule for yourself, start your day offline and be intentional about how you spend your time.

- To stay focused and avoid distractions, make it harder to indulge in sidetracking activities and redirect yourself frequently.

- To conquer isolation and loneliness, consider finding ways to share your expertise use mindfulness practices like breathing and being present in daily activities.

CHAPTER 3

Creating Your Workspace

The idea of working from anywhere sounds freeing, but finding a place where you can focus to do your best work is not always easy. Whether you want to use a dedicated home office or work from many different places, in this chapter we will review some of the most important things to consider to locate or create the best possible workspace for yourself.

3.1   Deep Work vs. Shallow Work

What is the best way to pick a place to work? If I were writing a chapter of a book, I would choose my home office. If I were sending a few emails, sitting at the kitchen table might work, too.

The best way to decide what type of environment you need is to consider whether your work is what author Cal Newport describes as **deep work**, which requires concentrated focus without distraction, or **shallow work**, which can be done with a lower level of concentration.[20]

For deep work, distractions of any size must be avoided because of a factor that University of Washington Bothell Professor Sophie Leroy calls "**attention residue**," where you're still thinking of a previous task as you're starting another one.[21]

Checking your phone for even an instant creates this attention residue; so does multitasking among various activities quickly. Deep work is best done in a distraction-free environment.

3.2	**The Ten Elements to Consider When Picking a Workspace**

In order to choose the best workspace (not a home office, which is covered in the next section), you need to consider the physical elements of the space along with the elements there that you can control in terms of privacy, technology, noise, and distractions. To help find the best workspace, you can download our handy checklist of *Ten Elements to Consider for Your Working Space*.

VISIT ONLINE RESOURCES FOR:
A checklist on elements to consider when picking a working space.

Here are the ten elements for you to consider:

1. **Distance** – How long will it take to commute and is the location convenient?

2. **Distractions** – How much external distraction is there from other people or activities?

3. **Amenities** – Does this space have meaningful amenities like food/coffee/gym or anything else you need?

4. **Human Connection** – Are there opportunities to connect with other people or meeting space and do you need this?

5. **Seating and Space** – Is there enough space and is the seating comfortable and varied (desks, couches, etc.)?

6. **Noise** – Is the noise level appropriate for your work (i.e., white noise versus distracting noise)?

7. **Cost** – How much will it cost in fees, food services, WiFi, parking, etc. in order to do your work there?

8. **Technology** – Is the WiFi fast enough, do you have access to a printer, or do you have other tech requirements?

9. **Privacy** – Do you have enough privacy for phone calls, screen sharing, or anything else you need to do?

10. **Security** – Who else will be around, is access restricted, and are you confident about your personal safety?

3.3	**Creating Your Home Office**

As entrepreneur and speaker Jeremiah Owyang suggests, "have a dedicated workspace (not on the bed) where you can conduct your business in a professional location." Whether you have a room or a repurposed closet, here are the elements to consider to ensure you're setting up the best possible home workspace.

→ **Atmosphere:** What does it take to do your best work? If you work best with natural light, try to find a space close to a window. If you like music while you work, set up a portable speaker. If your workspace changes temperature during the day, install an adjustable thermostat or get a space heater or a desk fan. Do what it takes to get the air around you to be the optimal temperature for you to do great work.

→ **Layout:** How will you set up your space so that you can enable some separation between work and life? Having a separate room for work is the easiest way to do this, but if you don't have the space, set aside a dedicated area that you don't use for anything except work. This will help you create the right mental separation not only to work when necessary, but also to let the work go when it's time to stop.

→ **Essentials:** What equipment is most important in your home office? It may be technology to communicate, a printer, or a bookshelf filled with resources to consult.

Whatever is most important, make sure it's available in your home office to maximize your productivity.

| 3.4 | **Setting Up Your Infrastructure** |

When you are working remotely, after creating a workspace, it is important to create a virtual infrastructure that allows you to work most effectively. This could include tools or platforms such as:

→ Scheduling tools and calendar apps

→ Productivity tools and software

→ Platforms for hiring virtual helpers or freelancers

→ File-sharing tools

→ Security or VPN services

→ Tools for sharing digital contracts

→ Financial and account platforms

→ Instant messaging tools

→ Project management software

→ Virtual meeting/collaboration tools

The choices for these tools can be overwhelming and costly, and you might wonder which (if any) of them you really need. If you're working for a company that dictates what tools to use, then your choice is easier or perhaps nonexistent.

3·5	**The Beauty of Analog**

About 15 years ago, when I worked in Australia, I bought a small painting of a frill-necked lizard from an Aboriginal artist. When I left the country and moved back to the United States, that painting came with me, and it has hung in every office I've had since.

It's a reminder of where I started my career, and the journey I took in my career to get to where I am today. We all have objects that are meaningful for us. When we start to work remotely, it can seem that there's no longer a place for them.

As you think about what it takes to create a great space to work remotely, remember to include those sentimental or meaningful objects that can help you feel more at home.

It may be a favorite coffee mug, a family picture, an inspiring book, or a unique painting. If it gives you comfort and helps you feel at ease, it's worth bringing with you, even if your workspace is just a temporary desk in a **co-working office**.

CHAPTER SUMMARY
KEY TAKEAWAYS:

- Consider these elements when picking a workspace: distance, distractions, amenities, human connection, space, noise, cost, technology, privacy, and security.

- Don't get overloaded with the vast number of tools you might use. Focus on what's most important.

- If you have physical objects that help you work better, bring them with you!

CHAPTER 4

Building Your Reputation and Personal Brand Virtually

When it comes to working virtually, your personal brand includes the way you portray yourself online and in virtual interactions. In this chapter, you will learn how to assess your current personal brand and how to improve it. To start, let's take a look at the definition of *personal brand* and why it matters.

4.1 What Is a Personal Brand?

A personal brand is the message that you share with the world about who you are before you walk into a room or join a virtual meeting. It is related to, but not the same as, your reputation.

Your personal brand is what you say about yourself, while your reputation is what others say about you.

PERSPECTIVE:
MITCH JOEL ON PERSONAL BRANDS

Your personal brand is the thinking behind the work. It's the knowledge, experience, and perspective that got you to where you are today.

Want to truly build a real and profound personal brand? Provide gifts. Gifts of knowledge. Gifts of information. Gifts of education. Make people come to you, because you are creating value by shining a light in an area that they need help with.[22]

– *Mitch Joel is an author, keynote speaker, and investor.*

Before I start sharing tips on how you can craft a stronger personal brand, let's consider a few reasons why it's worth focusing on it in the first place.

4.2 | Why Your Personal Brand Matters More When Working Virtually

A personal brand is valuable because it:

→ **Offers more independence.** In an uncertain time, a stronger personal brand gives the chance to build your reputation outside of your existing job title. This is hugely valuable for your career and network, both while performing your current job as well as for positioning yourself in the working world.

→ **Helps you be indispensable.** A more powerful personal brand can help you become more important at work. Superstars are the people most companies will work hardest to keep. Even if your company is reducing staff or your client is cutting its list of freelancers, a stronger personal brand can help you be the last to go.

→ **Gives you more credibility.** Having a strong personal brand can help you to walk into a new situation without needing to spend as much time introducing yourself or building credibility. The more people know about you before engaging with you, the better – because you can spend less time telling them why they should bother listening to you and more time providing real value.

→ **Makes you more money.** The simple fact of having a strong personal brand is that it gives you a higher profile and personal reputation, which in turn often lets you charge more for what you do or command a higher salary.

In my career, I have benefited greatly from having a personal brand. My blog helped me land my first book deal. My online presence helped me grow my profile as a professional keynote speaker. My published insights helped me launch two successful businesses.

Improving your personal brand virtually can do the same for you. Let's get started by exploring the three key components of a personal brand.

| 4.3 | **Three P's of a Powerful Personal Brand** |

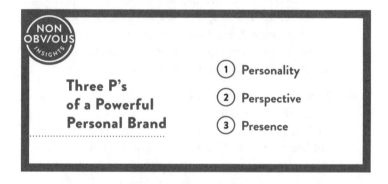

Here are the three key elements that matter for building a personal brand:

1. **Personality:** Who are you as a person, and how can you share your authenticity?

2. **Perspective:** What is your unique point of view, and how do you share it?

3. **Presence:** How visible are you online, and what do people see when Googling you?

4.4	**Demonstrate Your Personality**

In the real world, there are many ways to share our personality. It comes through in how we dress or what we choose to place on our desk. In the virtual world, this is harder to do.

To collect smart ideas for how to relay your personality in a virtual setting, I posed the question to my network on social media.

Here are a few of my favorite suggestions I got back:

→ Share a unique image for your avatar. (For years, my Twitter bio has had a cartoon LEGO man version of me. It has become my signature on that platform.)

→ Invite your pets to virtual meetings. They can turn a formal conference call into a more friendly meeting of minds. (*Contributed by Icy Sedgwick, freelance copywriter and host of the* Fabulous Folklore *podcast*)

→ Many video meeting platforms allow you to use a **virtual background**. While this can be fun, be sure to avoid making it too distracting. A word of caution: If you tend to move a lot, the background may not display properly.

→ When it comes to attire for virtual meetings, avoid busy and overbearing patterns that can become dizzying. Instead, opt for solid colors that complement your skin tone. Also, avoid white near your face, as it attracts light and can wash you out. Finally, dress in more fitted styles for a professional look. (*Contributed by Alicia Russman, owner/founder of Undeniable Boutique and Be Seen Branding*)

→ Before you start teaching and sharing what you know on your virtual session, start with a story to provide a personal and relevant experience that draws people into the conversation. (*Contributed by Mike Saporito, founder of Smart Habit*)

→ Lean into your personality – we're all unique and your audience will appreciate getting to know more about you, so maybe wear a bright color you like or sit in front of a shelf of your favorite things. (*Contributed by Evan Carroll, author and speaker*)

→ In virtual meetings, don't be afraid to show the real you. The kids or pets coming into the frame, a bit of a mess on your desk – it all helps people get to know you and connect with you when you're physically apart. (*Contributed by Scott Monty, strategic advisor and author of the* Timeless & Timely *newsletter*

→ Think about the full frame of your screen: What's behind you? Does the frame reveal who you are as a person? Does it evoke curiosity? Leave small hints of who you are so that it's easier for others to connect with you. (*Contributed by R/Lisa Zenno, ATCK cultural contributor*)

4.5   Bring Your Perspective

When I started speaking at conferences, I used to be on panels with several other speakers. The most common thing you heard on a panel was everyone agreeing with each other. That was boring and useless.

So I decided that my only goal would be to say something *different* from the other speakers. Sometimes I would intentionally try to disagree. Not in a mean way, but in a way that signaled to everyone in the audience that I had a unique perspective worth paying attention to.

I started doing the same thing virtually whenever I would write a blog post or share a tweet. Being different became a part of my personal brand, and it eventually led to the creation of the "non-obvious" brand itself. Having a unique point of view is an important part of standing out.

What makes you different from anyone else? It isn't always an easy question to answer, but asking it is an important piece of developing a better picture of what sets you apart.

4.6 Have a Presence Online

A year after college, I moved to Australia and landed my first job there because I had a website.

That was back in 1998, so having a personal website was unusual – but I got the job because of my answer to a single question the interviewer asked: "Did you build that website yourself?"

I said yes and got the job the next day.

At the time, the skill of designing a website and coding it in HTML was in demand.

> During the past decade, my personal website has helped me land future jobs and build a reputation for myself.

Of course, having a personal website isn't the only way to have a presence online. You can use social media to accomplish a lot of the same benefits.

This takes more than just sharing holiday photos or funny memes online, though. In my *Non-Obvious Guide to Marketing & Branding*,

I shared an approach to crafting a social media strategy for a small business that has useful lessons for individuals as well. You can download the full one-page template for how to craft your own strategy from the Online Resources for that book.

In that template, the biggest recommendation I share is to be intentional about which social media platforms you choose to use and why you are using each.

4.7	**The Importance of Consistency**

The final lesson in this chapter is the most important element of any successful brand: consistency.

> A good brand is always, always, always consistent.

If there is a fundamental truth to branding that any marketing expert will share with you, it is this. So across your platforms and wherever you choose to interact with people, make sure you're being as consistent as possible.

CHAPTER SUMMARY
KEY TAKEAWAYS:

- Your personal brand is what you say about yourself. Your reputation is what others say about you.

- Having a personal brand matters because it helps you build independence and credibility. Plus, it can help you make more money.

- The three P's of a powerful personal brand are personality, presence, and perspective.

- A good personal brand is always consistent.

PART TWO

Virtual Meetings

CHAPTER 5

How to Prepare for Virtual Meetings

Many of the basics about getting ready for a virtual meeting are the same as for an in-person meeting. You need to set a clear purpose and be intentional about whom you invite to the meeting.

Rather than spend more time on these basics, we will focus on some things you need to think about specifically when doing meetings virtually, starting with picking the right format.

5.1 The First Questions to Ask ...

In a world where people need to work in isolation, there is a growing temptation to have meetings when they may not be necessary and to overuse technology simply because it is available.

We didn't do this before, so why are we doing it now? The truth is that some meetings don't need to occur, and many don't need video.

Using video for every conversation is the virtual equivalent of getting on a plane every time you need to meet someone in a different city.

Here are a few critical questions to ask yourself before convening any virtual meeting:

1. Does this meeting really need to happen?

2. Who really needs to participate live?

3. Do we need video to collaborate?

4. What is the desired outcome of the meeting?

5. What is the ideal time? Are we considering multiple time zones for participants?

These may seem like basic questions, but it is amazing how often we fail to ask them simply because it's easy to schedule a virtual meeting at the click of a button.

5.2 Tips for Creating a Virtual Meeting Agenda and Purpose

The rules for creating an effective agenda for a virtual meeting aren't much different from those for a real-life meeting. Unfortunately, these rules aren't followed often enough for in-person meetings either. Here's a quick review with four tips that apply to all types of meetings, but matter even more when it comes to virtual meetings.

TIP 1 FOCUS ON WHAT'S MOST IMPORTANT

A good agenda isn't a lengthy list of everything that the meeting might cover. Prioritize the most important items and make sure you cover them first. That's especially true for action items that require decisions to be made in the meeting.

TIP 2 ASK PROVOCATIVE QUESTIONS

To generate the best discussion, particularly when people are not in the same room, consider circulating an agenda that consists of questions instead of a bulleted list of topics. Make the questions interesting and relevant enough that they will engage the participants.

TIP 3 SET REASONABLE TIMES

Try to be realistic about how long various topics will take and set clear ending points. Also, make sure everyone knows who hosts the meeting and who has the power to keep it moving from topic to topic.

TIP 4 GET STAKEHOLDER INPUT

The more you can involve the participants in crafting the agenda, the more involved they are likely to be in the meeting. Circulate your agenda early and look for buy-in from the people who matter most.

For more on this topic, read *The Non-Obvious Guide to Magical Meetings.*

5.3   Seven Rules of Virtual Meetings

From kids bursting into the room to people forgetting they are on video and doing embarrassing things, there are plenty of meeting-gone-wrong horror stories people love to share.

VISIT ONLINE RESOURCES FOR:
A shareable list of the seven rules.

Far more common, though, are a handful of annoying mistakes that happen often but can easily be prevented with a little education and some timely reminders. To avoid those, consider these Seven Rules of Virtual Meetings.

1. **Use the mute button.** If you aren't speaking, go on mute. If you are, go off mute. Practice so you don't mess this up. This is the most important rule.

2. **Be on time.** This is important for any meeting, but particularly for a virtual one because it's harder to stop and welcome latecomers in.

3. **Focus on the audio.** Virtual meetings aren't films. People usually need to hear you more than they need to see you. Get a headset or an external mic and test the sound to make sure it's good.

4. **Avoid backlighting.** Do not sit with a light or a window behind you. Try to find a spot where the light source is behind your camera shining on you instead – so you don't look like you are a silhouette from the witness protection program.

5. **Don't overshare.** Consider what people can see in the room behind you. Is it personal or potentially embarrassing? Be sure to remove any private information on your desktop before sharing your screen.

6. **Silence distractions.** Before the meeting, silence all alerts and notifications from your devices. Turn off any additional monitors

or other screen windows to avoid distractions, and close all unnecessary applications to improve your computer speed.

7. **Dress appropriately.** If it's a professional meeting, you should look professional. Working remotely is no excuse to look like you just rolled out of bed.

PERSPECTIVE:
LEN HERSTEIN ON MUTING YOURSELF

Think back to how you participate in phone conference calls. You probably muted yourself. And then, if, and only if, you had something to add, or you were asked a specific question, you unmuted yourself in order to participate.

Somehow, people have lost the ability to transfer that skill to video calls. I was on one the other day that had two presenters and over forty participants. The call was set up to be informational, yet most people left their video on. So we all got to see a whole load of people (in various states of dress and in backgrounds that included messy bedrooms) staring blankly at us.

Some left their microphones on, too – so we heard every sneeze ... and even one horrifying toilet flush.

Remember, there is nothing wrong with turning your video and microphone off if you are just there to observe. Then you can turn them on when you have something to add.[23]

– *Len Herstein is the founder of BrandManageCamp.*

5.4 Getting the Tech Right

The needs of the meeting should dictate the technology used, not vice versa. The first step is getting your tools right.

As Hassan Osman, author of *Influencing Virtual Teams*, suggests you should start by "investing in a good noise-canceling microphone. Unlike noise-canceling headphones, noise-canceling microphones help reduce ambient noises around you (such as kids crying or dogs barking) so that your meeting attendees couldn't hear them."

Beyond the hardware, you should think carefully about what platform you will use for meetings. As John Hall, co-founder of the Calendar scheduling and time management app, says, "Remote work success to me is all about having the right technology to manage your team and effectively work. I'm in a constant search for new tech that can help bring the best out of my remote team."

If you have the flexibility to choose new tools, it pays to be open-minded while seeking the latest tools that might be worth trying.

5.5	**Develop Your Participation Strategy**

In an in-person meeting, you can add ten minutes at the end of a presentation for Q&A and ask people to raise their hands. But participation requires more coordination and planning in a virtual meeting.

To develop your participation strategy, here are some useful questions:

→ Who needs to speak first to set the stage?

→ How familiar are all of your participants with the technology you are using?

→ When will the meaningful dialogue or discussion occur, and who will manage it?

→ What is the **backchannel** (the simultaneous online conversation outside the meeting), and who will be monitoring it and responding?

→ Are there individuals who could hijack the meeting or dialogue? If so, how will they be managed?

5.6 Four Models for Virtual Meetings

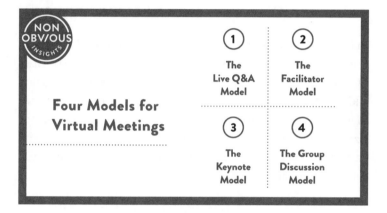

Once you settle your participation strategy, you can finalize an overall format for the meeting. Here are a few typical models to structure the meeting.

MODEL 1 THE FACILITATOR MODEL

In this model, a single facilitator serves as the host and moderates the entire session. This facilitator can hand off to several people to present or take control of what the audience sees at various points.

The key to using this model effectively is to choose a facilitator who is not only well-versed in the technology platform you are using, but also has the content knowledge to keep the meeting moving and prevent any single participant from derailing the flow.

MODEL 2 THE KEYNOTE MODEL

In this model, a single speaker presents in a keynote style while all other participants are silent observers. Webinars and executive-level presentations to a team are typically delivered in this style.

In this model, there isn't any real interaction. The key is to ensure the presenter has training or technical staff to manage the logistics of sharing the screen if necessary and to assure a high-quality audio connection. Remember audio is generally more important than video in almost every situation. Depending on the audience size, you might want a technical resource to help participants who have trouble getting into the meeting or experience any technical issues during the session.

MODEL 3 THE LIVE Q&A MODEL

This model may include a set presentation followed by a live Q&A session. Or perhaps just the Q&A session. In this model, you need someone who is skilled with the technology platform to collect questions and pose them to a single speaker or to give access to certain participants to pose their questions directly.

MODEL 4 THE GROUP DISCUSSION MODEL

The final model is an open discussion, where you may have three or more participants in your virtual video conference or session, and anyone can contribute at any time.

In this model, it is even more important to have a moderator because all the participants can speak whenever they want, and it can turn into chaos quickly. To manage this type of meeting, the moderator should have the ability to mute everyone to make a single announcement to them all or to interject strategically to keep the meeting moving forward.

5·7 Last-Minute Prep Tips

Assuming you have done everything else in this chapter to set up your meeting effectively and ensure that speakers know how to use the technology, here is a list of last-minute things to consider or check:

→ Test the technology at least an hour before the meeting to make sure it's stable for presenters and working as expected.

→ Prepare the room, especially if you are using video. Make sure that the portion of the room that will be visible looks good, the lighting is adequate, and the audio sounds good.

→ Send a reminder to participants, whether a day or an hour before the meeting, that includes details for how to dial in or log in for the meeting, so they don't need to search for it.

→ Don't forget to record the meeting if you plan to circulate the meeting afterward. And always let participants know if they will be recorded. Remember to hit the record button and double check that it starts!

→ Share your backup plan for the meeting. Make sure that your speakers know what to do if they have a problem and have your tech crisis card (a small note with the details of how to get technical help if necessary) ready with steps to follow, if needed.

CHAPTER SUMMARY
KEY TAKEAWAYS:

- Be intentional about whether you use video in meetings or not – and who you invite as well.

- Always follow the seven rules of virtual meetings: be on time, use the mute button, focus on the audio, avoid backlighting, don't overshare, silence distractions, and dress appropriately.

- Have a participation strategy to ensure people know how to contribute and who is leading.

CHAPTER 6

How to Foster Virtual Engagement

It is harder to engage anyone in a virtual setting. Everything that holds our attention in the real world, from body language to storytelling, is inherently more difficult when you can't be there in person. The virtual environment does offer some advantages, though.

What if you could manage the risk of distraction and the lack of personal connection and instead use the elements of a virtual meeting as an advantage? In this chapter, we will learn how to do that.

> The reason virtual meetings don't work is that most people never learn the skills to run them properly.

6.1   Five Reasons Virtual Meetings Suck

Many of us have spent too much time in virtual meetings that are a waste of time. I know I have, but I don't believe that virtual meetings or presentations need to be bad.

To improve your virtual meetings, let's start by highlighting a few of the most common reasons that virtual meetings go wrong:

PROBLEM 1   INCREASED DISTRACTIONS

Presenting the same thing you might have done in person in the same way doesn't work in a virtual session. People may face too many distractions and do other things at the same time.

PROBLEM 2   INTRUSIVE TECH

If you ever started a conference call with ten minutes of participants asking if you can hear them or trying to get their video working, you've already experienced intrusive tech. The fact is that much of the technology used for virtual sessions creates a lot of friction. People must download something, microphones don't work, and Internet connections fail.

PROBLEM 3 LACK OF AUDIENCE FEEDBACK

The laugh track for television sitcoms was created because the lack of an audience made producers worry that people wouldn't know when to laugh without the social cues from other audience members. In a live meeting, we can look to the people around us for a clue to how we might react. A virtual setting lacks this response, and we feel isolated in our reactions and find it's harder to engage – particularly when everyone else is on mute, creating an unnatural silence.

PROBLEM 4 NO ACCOUNTABILITY

When you are sitting in a live meeting, or you show up late, there are reputational and social costs to being tardy or using your phone during the meeting. Everyone else can see what you're doing. In a virtual session, there isn't any social pressure to keep you engaged or to prevent multitasking.

PROBLEM 5 ONE-WAY INTERACTION

Too often in virtual meetings, one person has a camera on and is delivering content while others are silently and invisibly listening. This creates an unbalanced meeting because one side has no insight into how the other side is reacting or if they are even engaging at all.

6.2	**How to Keep People Engaged**

How do we fix these issues?

It's easy to think that these problems are inevitable. After all, it's not reasonable to lock the doors of a virtual session or force everyone to appear on video to hold them accountable. And you certainly can't wish away technical issues just by hoping they don't happen.

Despite these difficulties, I have seen and used some techniques to encourage more engagement and address technology problems.

TIP 1 START WITH CONVERSATIONS

In the real world, you probably wouldn't start a meeting with all business. You would make some small talk and show you're a human. In a virtual setting, we may forget that it's just as important to do the same thing.

> Show interest in people first, and then get down to business.

Brie Reynolds, career development manager at FlexJobs, suggests to "spend the first five to ten minutes of any regular meeting on non-work conversation. Remote workers need to build in time to get to know each other on a more personal level to develop stronger relationships and feel connected."[24]

As Trendwatching Managing Director Henry Mason points out, "virtual meetings can often be super functional, as the medium isn't conducive to small talk. Don't let it strip out the humanity! Factor in some time for idle chit chat and everyone will come away feeling better connected."[25]

TIP 2 MAKE VIRTUAL TECH AN ADVANTAGE

If you know everyone who is participating will be on their computer during your meeting, a lot of possibilities open up. You can have them all visit a landing page directly to enter information. You can host and integrate a live poll. You can even tailor your content based on their immediate responses. Virtual meetings can enable faster real-time engagement if you can bake the interaction into the session.

TIP 3 USE MULTIPLE MEDIUMS/STYLES

While people may be able to sit through a 2-hour meeting or a 45-minute keynote, the rules are different for virtual sessions. In a world where people are used to 90-second YouTube videos, keeping their attention virtually can be more demanding. Sometimes I integrate more videos into virtual sessions or use interactive exercises asking participants to draw a picture or answer a question. You may even offer some time for engagement between participants.

These allow for a mental break and help audiences stay engaged longer because you are mixing up the content.

TIP 4 REDUCE THE FRICTION

Often the technology platform for a session is selected based on what platform is approved for a particular organization or what presenters are most comfortable using. Both are bad ways to choose technology. Instead, seek good answers. What tech would be easiest and fastest for your audience to get working? Who has the best live support to help people with issues? What tool doesn't require downloading? Considering the friction of the tech tools for your audience first can help prevent tech issues later.

TIP 5 ENCOURAGE UNDERVALUED VOICES

In a real-life meeting, you might avoid calling on people directly because it feels confrontational. In a virtual meeting, however, it can help keep a conversation moving and give some of the quieter voices a chance to share their perspective as well. As a recent article in the *New York Times* pointed out, women may not be getting an equal opportunity to contribute in meetings,[26] so facilitators need to work harder to help diminish the inherent bias toward women. If you can make a point to do this, you may find that you have more participation in a virtual session than you might have had if you had the same meeting in person.

TIP 6 EXPECT DISTRACTIONS

Just because your audience may have been distracted or multitasking doesn't mean that they are bad people or didn't want to hear your message. When presenting virtually, be more patient, keep it shorter, and find ways to keep them involved. Break up your content with chances for them to have input or ask questions.

TIP 7 HAVE A FOLLOW-UP PLAN

Perhaps even more than in-person meetings, the follow-up from a virtual session becomes much more important. If you recorded the session and promised to share it, make that happen quickly. If there are downloadable materials, make them easy to find and get. The moment right after a virtual session is critical to encourage engagement. This is a time when your audience may be most receptive to anything you can share. Plan the follow-up before the session and act on it quickly.

| 6.3 | How to Foster Creativity While Working Remotely |

Contributed by Kathryn Haydon, author of the Non-Obvious Guide to Being More Creative.

Creativity is often seen as a team sport when it comes to business. How can you be more creative when you are working remotely on your own?

At the office, we can experience creative collaboration in serendipitous water cooler conversations. Working from home, we have another opportunity for creative thought. It's what the science of creativity calls "incubation" time – when you're involved in a low-concentration activity and not directly focused on solving a particular challenge.

Many people say they get their most insightful thoughts while doing incubation activities like running, walking, driving, listening to music, or taking a shower.

The most creatively productive writers, scientists, and other greats in history made incubation time a non-negotiable part of their daily routines. Often this came in the form of a walk in nature, but for you it might be different.

Think back on the insights you've had over the past several months. Answer the following questions to help you choose your own ideal incubation activity.

VISIT ONLINE RESOURCES FOR:
An excerpt from the *Non-Obvious Guide to Being More Creative.*

When I get my highest-level insights and most fluid thoughts:

→ Am I outside or inside?

→ Am I moving or still?

→ What's the sound level? (Silence, white noise, music?)

→ Am I doing another activity, like cooking, building, writing, or drawing?

Incubation time is the silver lining of working from home. When we deliberately design it into our days, the result is more creativity with a side of work-life balance.

Kathryn Haydon is a speaker, innovation strategist, and the founder of Sparkitivity.

6.4	How to Facilitate a Virtual Meeting Like a Pro

Contributed by Douglas Ferguson and John Fitch, authors of the Non-Obvious Guide to Magical Meetings.

You can't just throw your usual meeting online. When going virtual, it is easy to let the fancy remote tools drive the purpose of your meeting. Instead, you want to think about your purpose and how it maps to the new virtual tools. You must reinvent your meetings.

We have a few meeting mantras that help us facilitate purposeful meetings. One of them is "work alone, together." A usual default with virtual workshops is to create a **digital whiteboard** (a collaborative space online where multiple people can contribute simultaneously) and let all the participants have at it. While this free-for-all approach may produce some results, it lets the power users of the tool hijack the workshop.

What about the more introverted participants? What about the person who is having a hard time adjusting to the new online tools?

You have to spend more time designing the experience for each of your virtual participants. Instead of just creating a virtual whiteboard or a digital wall with awesome tools such as MURAL, you also have to build digital tables and individual workstations so each participant can contribute with confidence. That is what we mean by "work alone, together."

VISIT ONLINE RESOURCES FOR:
An excerpt from the *Non-Obvious Guide to Magical Meetings*.

For example, we use MURAL to facilitate **Design Sprints**. We make sure that each participant has a digital workstation for each individual exercise within the Design Sprint. While we are all collaborating on the same digital wall, each participant is contributing in a way that is focused. They each get their own sandbox to play in.

In a virtual meeting space, you need to invest extra time prepping the environment where each meeting participant will work alone.

Doing the work in the meeting is everyone's responsibility, so you must decentralize the exercises in a manner that will occupy each participant. A virtual meeting expert ensures that each participant has a clear responsibility at any moment. Otherwise, you probably will lose them to the distractions on their computer.

One final technique to consider when facilitating virtual meetings is using any special features your technology platform might allow to create breakout rooms or subdivisions in your meeting. These types of segmented conversations can be highly effective to break up a larger group into smaller working teams and help foster more concentrated discussions.

When using this type of feature, it is important to be clear with the goals of the session and also to be specific about how these breakouts are meant to come back and rejoin the group.

CHAPTER SUMMARY
KEY TAKEAWAYS:

- Virtual meetings can be filled with distractions and intrusive tech. Minimize these problems by reducing the friction and focusing on making it more engaging.

- To facilitate a virtual meeting like a pro, ensure that each participant has a clear responsibility at any moment.

- To be more creative while working remotely, consider activities like running, listening to music, or otherwise taking a break from the constant pressure of work.

CHAPTER 7

How to Deliver a Virtual Presentation

For three years, I taught presentation skills and storytelling at Georgetown University. At the time, learning to present virtually was an afterthought. Since then, this skill has become much more important not only to teach my students, but also to employ when delivering virtual presentations myself.

In the past few years, I probably have presented virtually more than a hundred times. Thanks to several event cancellations, in the past 30 days alone I have done 15 virtual presentations, training sessions, or webinars. The hardest thing about them is delivering an engaging talk without having live audience feedback.

As a speaker, when you can't see your audience react, it can feel like an impossible task to try and create engagement.

In this chapter, you will learn some of the fundamentals for what does and doesn't work when presenting remotely. They will help you ace doing virtual presentations, no matter how often you need to do them.

7.1	**Getting the Setup Right**

There is no single way to set up your space to deliver a virtual presentation. However, knowing a few of your choices and the logistics involved can help ensure that your setup isn't a distraction for your audience, but rather helps you present in the best possible way.

Beyond the obvious basics, like testing the technology, here are a few simple tips to ensure you are set up to deliver a successful presentation:

1. **Get to eye level.** When your computer is on the desk in front of you with the camera angled up, you'll appear as if you're looking down. Instead, put your computer on a stack of books to bring your camera to eye level. It makes a big difference.

2. **Follow the seven rules.** The seven rules for virtual meetings shared in Section 5.3 are even more important when you're presenting. Get the audio right, make sure you're not accidentally sharing personal information, avoid backlighting, silence your devices, and follow all the other rules, too.

3. **Invest in professional tools.** Depending on how often you are presenting virtually, you may want to invest in some tools to make your setup more professional. This includes a better microphone, upgraded camera, appropriate lighting and an uncluttered background.

4. **Know your model and participation strategy.** In Chapter 5, we looked at the various models for virtual meetings and how to structure a participation strategy. When presenting, you need to ensure you have thought about both issues and have a clear approach on how you'll handle them.

7.2	**Ten Tips for Effective Virtual Presenting**

The biggest question I am asked is whether presenting virtually requires a different approach than presenting in real life. The short answer is yes.

VISIT ONLINE RESOURCES FOR:
An easy to share list of my Ten Tips for Effective Virtual Presenting.

Here are some of the most common tips I have recently shared with people to help them conquer the unique challenges of doing a presentation virtually.

TIP 1 MAKE IT SHORTER

At first, I used to try and translate my usual 45-minute keynote into a virtual session. It didn't work. Holding attention is harder in a virtual setting, so start with your most powerful points, share only what you really need to, and keep your presentation as short as you can.

TIP 2 MIX IT UP

Can you use a mix of visuals, props, and video? What about incorporating a virtual poll? The nice thing about presenting virtually is that you have an opportunity to use the technology to add a variety of methods to engage your audience. Though many of them do add a bit of technical complexity, it is often worth the effort because it makes your presentation more memorable. As Idea Enthusiast founder Greg Roth notes, "the biggest thing we may be losing in an all-remote work world is the power of visual thinking. Team leaders should emphasize sketching, speaking visually (anecdotes, analogies, etc.), and sharing powerful visuals."[27]

TIP 3 DOUBLE THE ENERGY

Without an audience, you will have to work extra hard to bring energy to your presentation so it doesn't feel flat. It is much easier to bring energy if you allow yourself to move. If you can, consider presenting while standing up.* At least use your hands or arms in gesturing. Making sure your energy shows through in how you present. As a general rule, when you feel like you're overdoing it with your energy level, you probably have it just right.

*Note/Confession – This is a rule I strategically ignore. Watch a short video in the online resources to learn why.

TIP 4 LOOK AT THE CAMERA, NOT THE PEOPLE

On a virtual call, you may be tempted to present to the room or people you can see. The problem is, when you do that, it will seem like you are looking sideways. Instead, look directly at your camera. It will seem unnatural not to look at your audience, but when you look at the camera it will appear as though you are looking at the people watching.

PERSPECTIVE:
MARK BOWDEN ON EYE CONTACT

Look people in the eye. One way to do that is to draw a smiley face on a post-it note and then you post that on top of your camera and it just attracts your attention to the camera and gives you that smile which your instinct easily gravitates towards and repeats back that smile. It just means I pay more attention to the camera than I do my own image.[28]

– *Mark Bowden is a human behavior and body language expert.*

TIP 5 SKIP THE RHETORICAL QUESTIONS

Questions that don't require an answer or require people to raise their hand to answer don't work in a virtual environment. They just end up making people feel silly, and you look out of touch. Skip the questions, rhetorical or otherwise, unless you're actually integrating a poll to allow people to do a live vote.

TIP 6 BRING THE HUMANITY

How can you inject your personality into your talk and make it more human? Perhaps you incorporate a picture of yourself with your family. Or you let them see your home office behind you on screen. Or you integrate a prop as part of your talk. Any way you can, try to make your talk more personal so people can feel connected to you.

PERSPECTIVE:
LAURA GASSNER OTTING ON GREEN SCREENS

Frankly, I hate green screens. Your efforts to hide who you are leave me lonelier than before. It's not that I realize I don't know you. It's that I realize you never wanted me to in the first place. That's not a recipe for trust.

Instead, I'd like to see your bookshelf. I'd like to see your 5K medals. I'd like to see your family pictures. I'd like to see your puppy. I'd like to see you. Show me your human side, and I'll show you mine.[29]

– *Laura Gassner Otting is the author of* Limitless: How to Ignore Everybody, Carve Your Own Path, & Live Your Best Life.

TIP 7 REPEAT MAIN POINTS

When listening to a virtual presentation, I have found that my attention tends to wander, and I anticipate this from my audience as well. To make sure they don't miss my most important points, I usually find a way to repeat them more often than I might when presenting in person, and I remind people they can always take a screen grab or email me to get my slides later.

TIP 8 USE MORE TEXT

When you are doing a virtual presentation, the chances are people are sitting right next to their screens. This gives you an opportunity to use slides with more text than you ordinarily would in a stage presentation. This doesn't mean you should fill your slides with 8-point font, but the general rule of 24-point font as a minimum for presentations can be lower for a virtual presentation. As long as the text you're sharing is valuable, having a bit more of it on screen can help reiterate your point without detracting from the flow.

TIP 9 TALK SLOWER (OR PAUSE MORE)

Everyone has a tendency to speak faster when presenting – sometimes even more so when presenting virtually. The immediate solution is just to slow down. An alternative is learning how to use pausing in your pace to make your presentations more effective.

PERSPECTIVE:
MICHAEL PORT ON PAUSING

Instead of slowing down, focus on pausing. Speakers who speak too slowly have a soporific effect. I speak quickly. But I pause at the right places. That creates rhythm. I slow down when it serves the speech to slow down. Audiences can easily absorb the important points if you give them pause time.[30]

– Michael Port is the founder of Heroic Public Speaking.

TIP 10 FOLLOW UP QUICKLY

When you promise something as a follow-up, you always want to share it. However, audience expectations when it comes to a virtual presentation are higher. Since your audience members are already sitting there on their computers or phones participating and listening, they often expect you will share any follow-up materials right away. To accommodate, I will often schedule an email to send right as my presentation concludes – or direct participants to a landing page online where they can download relevant materials right away. The longer I can provide value and keep their engagement, the more memorable my insights can be.

7.3 How to Add Variety to Your Virtual Presentation

A virtual presentation works best if you have some variety around the content that you are presenting. What does this variety look like? Here are a few things you might incorporate into your presentation to add more variety and interest for your audience:

→ Move the camera (or yourself).

→ Switch among external videos and visuals.

→ Integrate polls, surveys, or other interactive features.

→ Bring a guest to break up the flow and add interest. You can get creative here. For example, I recently read that you can hire a farm animal to join your next virtual meeting!

→ Use a virtual background purposefully. Just remember that these can appear disjointed if you tend to move a lot, so use this with care.

More than in-person presentations, you need to mix it up in virtual sessions and offer more breaks and reminders.

7.4	**Making Your Presentation Memorable Virtually**

Contributed by Dr. Carmen Simon, author of Impossible to Ignore.

After helping others create and deliver thousands of business presentations, I am noticing a trend toward substance abuse: we sometimes provide too little information, thinking we are doing audiences a favor; or we provide too much unfiltered information. Both extremes have a negative impact on influencing memory, which means a negative impact on influencing decisions. How do we fix this?

TIP 1 AVOID FORCED BREVITY

Brevity often breeds superficiality. Does it bother you when some people impose: "You have to present topic X and can only do it in three slides"? That's sheer nonsense, and it drives me crazy. Can you see the potential flaw in: "We are looking for some simple rules on topic Y"? Some fields are immensely complex and there are no simple rules. I recently heard a presentation on "three simple steps to overcome depression." If this was so simple, we would all skip around with daisies in our hands.

Many topics are complicated and situational. Don't oversimplify them and don't agree to take two minutes to address a topic that needs 30 minutes of explanation.

Here's a truth that many miss: to build memory traces in someone's brain, you need some complexity. Your brain won't appreciate simplicity unless it also sees the complexity from which it came. Plus, simplicity becomes a snoozer after a while, which leads to lack of attention, which leads to lack of memory.

TIP 2 ASSUME ACCOUNTABILITY

Often, we sacrifice complexity and stay on the surface "because the client/boss asked for it that way." These circumstances erode individual accountability. It is tempting to blame the environment ("Marketing told us to do it this way") because it absolves us of any personal responsibility. The problem with this victim mentality is that the more we believe we don't have control over our environment, the more undisciplined we become. I strongly urge you: Do not join the generation of "whatever" people. Find messages you believe in and don't compromise on the amount of depth you need to do them justice.

TIP 3 BALANCE ACTION WITH REFLECTION

We give our audiences too little or too much unfiltered information because we are often in a rush. The hurried lifestyle of customers and supervisors pushes us to deliver quickly, often sacrificing balance and validity. Because of time constraints, we bypass discipline and look for shortcuts.

> Developing content too fast is like vacuuming too fast: you miss stuff.

Before you share content with others, reserve enough time to share your thoughts with those you consider your guardians for depth, validity, and reliability. When you share content from this position, and offer something meaningful – not superficial – you will earn one of the greatest gifts of all: a spot in someone's mind.[31]

Carmen Simon, PhD, is the founder of Memzy and author of several books on how to create memorable content for presentations.

PERSPECTIVE:
USING VISUALS TO MAKE IDEAS SHAREABLE

One of my favorite techniques for visuals is to repeat a few key ones and make them available as downloads to make the idea more shareable. I call these *stealable slides.*

– *From the Author*

7.5   How to Sell with a Virtual Presentation

The hardest kind of meeting for many people to do virtually is a sales presentation. The lack of audience feedback and inability to read the room seem like deal killers. They certainly make it harder.

When you have no alternative, though, there are some things you can do to make your virtual pitch as strong as possible.

1. **Set ground rules** – If everyone knows how to interact with the tools you're using, you can make interaction more likely. Show your prospect how to use the chat feature and make sure the technology isn't a barrier to engagement.

2. **Ask them what format they prefer** – It's tempting to go into a virtual sales presentation and launch straight into PowerPoint. Doing that robs your prospects of giving you important direction up front. Instead, start the meeting by confirming how they would like the meeting to go. Do they prefer that you present slides or just have a conversation? Letting them choose puts the decision in their hands and shows that you're not afraid to be flexible to work in the way that is best for them.

3. **Start with what's most important** – In a real-life presentation, you have more license to build up to a big reveal. In a virtual meeting, you risk distractions or losing their attention faster

– so bring your best insights and most compelling messages up front and share them earlier. That way if they do check out (mentally or physically), they won't miss the best part.

4. **Tell a better story** – The best sales presentations offer a vision for a potential future that is appealing. If you can get your prospect to imagine that future during your presentation by telling them a powerful story to paint that picture, you are much more likely to be successful.

5. **Don't blame the tech** – If things aren't going well, it's easy to blame the technology or make excuses. Instead of doing that, be proactive and handle issues that may arise in a positive and confident way.

PERSPECTIVE:
WEBEX TEAM ON SCREEN SHARING

Your team puts a lot of time into creating and personalizing sales presentations; screen sharing ensures that those efforts don't go to waste. Everyone in the screen sharing session can view documents together. Multimedia can help add dynamism to a sales presentation, and graphical elements presented through screen sharing can help illustrate numbers that lack life on a traditional sales call, as well as reinforce benefits.[32]

7.6 Why Apologies Kill Virtual Presentations

Contributed by Dr. Carmen Simon, author of **Impossible to Ignore.**

I was just listening to a presenter at a conference who started this way, "I am so sorry this presentation is right before lunch."

When you apologize, you are asking your audience for leniency; you are asking them to expect a poorer presentation. You are also destroying your credibility before you have a chance to demonstrate you have it. And, given that the brain might remember firsts and lasts better than the middle of a sequence, an audience might remember you for the wrong reasons.

> Never apologize before you begin your presentation.

Avoid these phrases if you want to be memorable for the right reasons: "I'm sorry the meeting software is slow," "I apologize we started late," "I am sorry the text on the slides is so small ..."

But what if you did start a little late and the meeting software had problems and the slides are even worse? Simply address the problem, tie it to what you want people to remember, and move on.

For example, let's imagine someone gave you really complex and text-intensive slides to present. Say something like, "Even though the slide is convoluted, it reminds us that the product offers a lot of capabilities and substance." [Quickly click to the next slide.] If all slides are like that, black out the projector and have a conversation with your audience instead.

Avoid tentative phrases when you start a presentation too. Questions such as "Can you hear me OK?" or "Can you see these slides OK?" or "Let's see, where shall I start?" don't do justice to what you want people to remember.

> A bit of self-deprecating humor is OK when you keep it succinct and tie it to a topic instead of using it just for the sake of using humor.

Avoid demeaning yourself in a presentation. Never make comments like, "I'm not very good at ..." or "I suppose I should have known this slide was here." Demeaning yourself destroys your credibility, weakens your presentation, and is uncomfortable for your audience.

Picture a beginning like this: "I used to have the body of a football player. Now I have the body of a fantasy football player. And this is what I am noticing in our software development too: sometimes we let fantasy cloud our judgment. Here's what I am recommending to trim down our fantasy feature list ..."

Avoid short, introductory expressions that ask participants to be tolerant or understanding about your topic. "I'm not an expert in this field but ..." or "I'm not a CEO but ..." Phrases like these prime the listener to devalue or question what you are about to say.

> Overall, look at your beginnings as ways to prime the brain for what's to come.

Priming means that we can use a stimulus to influence how the brain interprets the next stimulus. A weak beginning offers the wrong prime and you have to work a lot harder to recover from it as the presentation unfolds. A strong beginning offers a strong prime. And when you prime your audiences' brains the right way, you don't have to work so hard during every single minute of your presentation.

Create a strong association between your content and sub-sequent triggers and you will be consistently and effortlessly on people's minds.[33]

CHAPTER SUMMARY
KEY TAKEAWAYS:

- When presenting virtually follow these quick tips to improve how you look and sound: face a window, invest in a high-quality microphone, and adjust your camera to eye level.

- To keep your audience's attention when presenting virtually – keep it short, mix it up, make eye contact, and double your energy level.

- More effectively sell in a virtual presentation by setting ground rules, asking what format they prefer, and telling a better story.

- Maximize your credibility in virtual presentations by using self-deprecating humor, avoiding apologizing, and creating strong associations between your content and subsequent triggers.

CHAPTER 8

Virtual Events, Trainings, Webinars, and More

Beyond virtual meetings between team members or business colleagues, growing numbers of events are being held virtually as well.

In this section, you will learn how to navigate this expanding world of virtual events, whether you want to join one as a participant or host one of your own.

8.1 What Is a Virtual Event?

A virtual event is any gathering of people other than a meeting that can be used to inspire, train, inform, or otherwise engage. These include remote training sessions, online educational sessions such as webinars, distance learning initiatives, and even full-scale virtual conferences with avatars and simulated virtual-reality event spaces. One category we probably will see much more often is the **hybrid event** – a description for events that have both in-person and virtual ways for speakers and attendees to participate. This category is poised for big growth as people re-evaluate which events they will travel to and which they will be content to join virtually.

8.2	Six Types of Virtual Experiences (and When to Use Them)

Six Types Of Virtual Experiences

1. Webinars
2. Online Training
3. Virtual Offsites
4. Virtual Conferences
5. Augmented Reality
6. Virtual Reality

We already have talked about virtual meetings and presentations. Let's consider a few other types of virtual experiences you may encounter:

→ **Online training/master classes:** These are usually on-demand modules available to help someone learn about a new topic. They can cover anything from teaching technical skills such as coding to getting a lesson on playing the guitar. Use this when you need to deliver education accessible on demand.

→ **Webinars:** Similar to online trainings, webinars usually are hosted as a live event and recorded to watch afterward. Since they typically are delivered live, webinars often incorporate discussion or Q&A sessions with the speaker or between participants. Use this when you need to build momentum for a new product or service or share thought leadership with a live audience.

→ **Virtual offsites:** When you bring a team together virtually to discuss core business issues or strategy, it is a virtual offsite. The key for such sessions is to have a good integrated method of collaboration so all members can contribute their perspectives to discussions. Use this when you need to bring your team together and cannot include everyone in person.

→ **Virtual conferences/trade shows/expos:** These are experiences created primarily to connect buyers and sellers in a particular category or to share insights from experts. Some can be highly interactive, where participants create their own avatars and physically move through the space in a 3D-generated way. Use this when you want to bring buyers and sellers together without the significant cost, effort, and time required to host a live in-person event.

→ **Augmented reality** (**AR**): The simplest way to describe AR is as a technology that overlays graphics, animations, or text onto what you are seeing in the real world. This could include information that "unlocks" when you point your phone's camera at a code or location. Use this when you want individual people to experience a different sort of immersion with what they already are seeing.

→ **Virtual reality** (**VR**): The types of experiences you can have in this category are growing quickly. At the moment, all VR experiences require you to wear a headset in order to place yourself inside an imagined reality. Some have sensors and therefore allow a more immersive world you can explore in 360 degrees, while others offer a flatter experience. Use this when you can create an experience or use an existing one to help immerse your audience and give them a memorable perspective.

8.3 How to Produce a Virtual Event

Contributed by Andrea Driessen, author of The Non-Obvious Guide to Event Planning.

With so much of our lives online, the virtual or hybrid experience you're producing must deliver true value to compete with all the other available choices. Here are some tips on how to do it.

TIP 1 PRELOAD THE FUN

When promoting a virtual event, seed messaging with a few practical insights and content-driven teasers. These can build buy-in and foster a feeling of exclusivity. That way, registrants don't just learn when your event's happening; they have even more reasons to attend.

TIP 2 PLAN CONTENT BEFORE PLATFORM

First, choose the content you want to communicate, and then choose your platform of content delivery technology.

TIP 3 START WITH BEST FIRST

On the day of your event, optimize attention by beginning with your very best, most enticing, carefully scripted content. Dive right into your most compelling ideas. These are never sponsor-related remarks or profuse thank-yous. If you're recording the programming, superb content ensures the footage can be used in promotional teasers for the next event. (See what you missed?!)

TIP 4 TRANSFORM PASSIVITY INTO ACTIVITY

If you're not planning to add interactivity, you should reconsider migrating online. Your "experience" may be better and more simply communicated via email. Build engagement beyond a simple chat box by ensuring that content includes varied interactivity. Try quizzes and contests before, during, and after. Use audience polling and integrate Q&A time and whiteboarding. Choose a platform in which your presenter can highlight and draw in real time. Play music and video. Close with a pithy, practical summary and a strategic call to action to end on a high note.

TIP 5 REMEMBER: LESS IS MORE

Your virtual guests will remember more when you remember to keep the agenda streamlined. The best online meetings or meeting segments are short: 30 minutes or less. Focus on just two or three important messages and takeaways, and design every agenda element around those outcomes.

TIP 6 BOOST THE AFTERGLOW

After virtual or hybrid events, hold smaller online meetups so attendees can continue connecting, learning, networking, and boosting accountability. This also can enhance in-person event attendance over time as relationships crystallize.

TIP 7 DELIVER DATA-DRIVEN RESULTS

An inherent benefit of virtual events is easy tracking of virtual attendance, participant retention rates, and your most click-worthy content. Take advantage of this built-in ROI richness so you can prove value to your stakeholders and make measurable improvements over time.

VISIT ONLINE RESOURCES FOR:
An excerpt from the *Non-Obvious Guide to Event Planning*.

TIP 8 CREATE MORE KA-CHING

Record your meatiest virtual meetings so you can reuse the footage for new hire training, social media posts, sponsor acquisition, video blogs, and **sizzle reels** that sell future events.

8.4 How to Select a Virtual Speaker

Contributed by Andrea Driessen, Author of The Non-Obvious Guide to Event Planning.

Whether speakers are in person or virtual, they must project authenticity, trustworthiness, and confidence. However, these qualities are often more difficult to convey when a live audience isn't present.

The reciprocal energy, eye contact, enthusiasm, modulation, and feedback that normally emerge from a live audience in a room are lacking in virtual events. That's why online presenters need to be evaluated and selected differently.

Here are my top four questions to consider as you evaluate potential speakers to select one who will be able to bring energy and really deliver in a virtual context.

QUESTION 1 CAN THEY BREAK THE FOURTH WALL?

The best speakers build relationships with each individual by looking right into the camera, according to virtual speaker coach Dia Bondi. This is a nonobvious and trainable skill for most speakers. Unlike humans in a live audience, a camera doesn't give feedback. Speakers must learn to create connection with people they can't see.

QUESTION 2 IS THE ENERGY LEVEL RIGHT?

Look for a speaker who can deliver a talk with a wider vocal range and greater inflection than others might normally. Monotone is a buzzkill online, where attention spans are extremely low to begin with.

QUESTION 3 DO THEY INCORPORATE VARIETY?

The speaker should be accustomed to replacing boring data dumping and switching up the spoken word with music, Q&A, quizzes, relevant stories, polling, and fast-paced clicks through elegant, easy-to-read slides.

VISIT ONLINE RESOURCES FOR:
A guide to selecting a speaker.

QUESTION 4 WILL THEY DO THE PREP WORK?

You must be able to count on the speaker to participate in pre-event training and a rehearsal using all intended technology. This should include a thorough equipment check in the same way you would if your event were in person.

Andrea Driessen is the Founder and Chief Boredom Buster at No More Boring Meetings.

8.5 Three Tips for Crafting Virtual Experiences That Engage People

Contributed by Jay Baer, founder of Convince & Convert and bestselling author.

Just like face-to-face events, several success factors typically determine whether virtual events are magical or mediocre.

TIP 1 SHORTEN SESSION LENGTHS

It is far more difficult to hold an audience's attention in a virtual event. We created the concept of a "Webinine" – a webinar that lasts just nine minutes. The audience show-up rate is much higher.

We're not suggesting that every session be just nine minutes, but consider shortening the time slots you would use for a physical event by 15 or 30 minutes.

TIP 2 SHARPEN YOUR TITLES AND DESCRIPTIONS

In a physical event setting, attendees often rely on word of mouth, asking other participants which breakout they are attending and why. Most virtual conferences lack this dynamic, so participants in your virtual event have less information when deciding which sessions to tune in for and which to skip.

It is even more important to use clear and compelling session titles and descriptions for your virtual conference programming.

TIP 3 USE A MODERATOR OR AN EMCEE

In a face-to-face event, the moderator or emcee helps contextualize the information presented and keep energy up.

In virtual events, having a consistent face and voice that "stitches together" the virtual sessions for participants adds much-needed familiarity and helps alleviate the isolated feeling that online events sometimes produce.[34]

Jay Baer is the founder of Convince & Convert and the author of multiple bestselling books.

8.6 Non-Obvious Ideas for Virtual Experiences

The world of virtual events is transforming, and many organizations are getting more experimental in producing them – particularly since the COVID-19 crisis. To see where the world of virtual events may be headed, consider this smart compilation of "eVents" that the team of researchers at PSFK, an insights platform that tracks retail, fashion, and consumer trends, put together:

→ **Ready-player platforms:** Look beyond current video portals and video conferencing technologies and consider sports, gaming, and social platforms.

→ **Influencer exclusives:** Invite social media influencers to record and share content from your stages and other event experiences.

→ **Insider reporting:** Ask employees to act as reporters from the event and share content.

→ **Overload information:** Augment the live viewing experience with additional information and stats or offer a second screen experience for phones or tablets.

→ **Instant build:** Create features that enable the audience to add to the learning experience. Attendees could contribute by providing written, video, and audio content at a click of a button.

→ **Embedded attendee:** Allow virtual attendees to sit anywhere – even on the stage. eSports fans already have the option to view games from multiple viewpoints, even from within the theater of the game itself.

→ **Use data to connect:** Connect like-minded people in the audience by matching profiles. Use this approach to help sponsors pinpoint the right attendees to interact with.

→ **Watch parties:** Coordinate virtual and real-life meeting spaces that help people watch your event together. These gatherings help attendees focus on the content and interact to build on what they learn.

→ **Create team challenges:** Build virtual teams out of the audience and speakers, and set tasks and challenges throughout the event.

→ **Make them play:** Keep the audience engaged and motivated by mixing the content up with activities between and sometimes during main sessions. Consider running contests, virtual games, and even karaoke!

→ **Augment the attendee:** Provide content that could enhance the way the attendee appears to the others. Share branded background videos to play in video-conference calls; then send exclusives as prizes when they win!

→ **Sell stuff:** Let people buy things from you, both physical and virtual. Some of the most successful live-streaming companies are eCommerce retailers.

→ **Gift exchange:** Provide a mechanism for attendees to reward speakers, event organizers, and other attendees with monetary gifts, and other tokens.[35]

PERSPECTIVE:
THE NON-OBVIOUS BEYOND DIVERSITY SUMMIT

What would it take to create a more inclusive world? In early 2021, my team hosted an ambitious gathering of more than 200 speakers across 54 sessions to have a wide-ranging conversation about how to create a more inclusive world.

Topics at the summit included women in tech, disability at work, inclusive gaming

representation in politics, neurodiversity, ageism, inclusive casting, diverse museum experiences, racial literary, rural broadband, funding minority entrepreneurs,

respecting indigenous culture and more.

To watch a behind the scenes video and learn more about the summit and how it all came together, visit www. nonobviousdiversity.com.

– From the Author

CHAPTER SUMMARY
KEY TAKEAWAYS:

- Events will increasingly go hybrid, offering a mix of in-person and virtual sessions and experiences for live and online participants.

- The most common types of virtual events or experiences are webinars, online trainings and master classes, virtual offsites, virtual showrooms and trade shows, augmented reality, and virtual reality.

- To better engage people in virtual events, use shorter sessions, sharpen titles and descriptions, and use a moderator or an emcee to contextualize the event.

- When selecting a virtual speaker, make sure they have the right energy level and offer a variety of ways to engage.

PART THREE

Virtual Collaboration

CHAPTER 9

The Art of Virtual Communication

Given how often we do it, we all should be experts in virtual communications such as emails and instant messaging. Yet for all the time we spend communicating, most of us haven't had much training on how to do it well.

In this chapter, we will look at the biggest common mistakes that people make when communicating virtually and how to fix them. We also will look at how to collaborate with people you have never met, what you should know about **digital body language**, and how to avoid overcommunicating with digital tools.

9.1 Why Virtual Collaboration Is Hard

I remember taking a tour of the MIT Media Lab and passing an empty couch with a live video feed in front of it. On the other end of the video was a similar couch in the European outpost of the Media Lab in Ireland. The idea of the live video was to enable real- time collaboration with peers from across the ocean. Anyone could come sit and have a conversation with anyone on the other end. It was brilliant. Unfortunately, as my brother who worked there told me, on most days that couch was usually empty.

> It turns out that having the technology for connection doesn't magically make connection happen.

In fact, more often than not technology stands in the way of those connections happening because the interactions feel disjointed or artificial.

Visit online resources to watch my interview with Tom fishburne (marketoonist) about his creative process!

© marketoonist.com

How do we avoid those technological barriers and find better ways to collaborate when we can't be there in person? The first important step is to focus on the type of communication we want to have.

| 9.2 | **Setting Expectations with Your Virtual Team** |

When it comes to communicating with someone in a virtual way, there are generally two methods: synchronous and asynchronous.

Speaking to someone on the telephone or live in a virtual meeting is an example of **synchronous communication**. Sending an email is an example of **asynchronous communication**.

This seems obvious, but the problem is that there are many forms of virtual communication sitting squarely in between. Take a text message, for example.

What is a reasonable amount of time to wait for a response to a text? Ten seconds? Five minutes?

Your answer may be different than what a colleague would say, and within that gap is the potential for misunderstanding and conflict.

PERSPECTIVE:

ILMA NAUSEDAITE ON ASYNCHRONOUS COMMUNICATION

Our whole communication is totally asynchronous, and because of that you can plan your day and week ahead. It's really connected with productivity and why we can work faster as a team just because of that mindset. No one will interrupt you.

I think having a team that is in deep flow, in deep work is much more important than just putting out fires.[36]

– *Ilma Nausedaite is the COO of Mailerlite.*

Luckily, there are a few techniques to help you to manage this challenge and set better expectations.

TIP 1 SET WORK CULTURE GUIDELINES

The best way to manage the potential for conflict is for a leader at work to set clear expectations on the team's virtual work culture. What are the standard working hours? Are people expected to respond or check emails on the weekend? When people don't know what's expected, they create their own expectations. Make it easier for everyone and set expectations centrally.

PERSPECTIVE:
DHARMESH SHAH'S PAJAMA PRINCIPLE

Remember that remote people are people. Treat them with the same care that you do anyone else in the team. And you can dramatically open up the pool of possible talent that you have access to just by letting the best people do their best work. And often their best work is done when they are in their pajamas. The Pajama Principle is simple. It states that your success is proportional to the degree to which you let people stay in their pajamas. I live by the Pajama Principle, both as a beneficiary and an implementer."[37]

– Dharmesh Shah is the CTO of HubSpot.

TIP 2 TRAIN YOUR TEAMMATES

Aside from having a centrally dictated set of expectations, you have a personal responsibility to train your teammates on what to expect from you in terms of communication. How quickly you choose to respond to requests or engage in virtual communications sets expectations for the next time. Do you agree to meetings right away? Do you pick up the phone any time it rings? Do you respond to emails at 11 p.m.? Each time you do any of these things, remember that you are setting the new expectation for next time.

TIP 3 ACKNOWLEDGE NOW, RESPOND LATER

One of my favorite techniques to help manage expectations from my team and my clients is to respond quickly. I acknowledge receiving their email or request, and I say I will be getting back to them. This offers the best of both worlds: They get a response fast and know that their message was received. I don't have to drop everything else I'm doing to address their need right away. Also, I avoid unintentionally setting their expectations for an immediate solution the next time.

9.3	How to Mind Your Digital Body Language

Contributed by Erica Dhawan, founder of Cotential.

Digital body language involves the new hidden cues and signals in our digital conversations. We all know that most communication is through body language. Today, things have changed. We're often in virtual teams.

Do we understand the new cues and signals of "virtuality"? I have a few best practices to help people make sure that they're learning more about their own digital styles. One is that timing is everything.

Often what we see is that people respond 24/7. Some people expect that; others never would dream of it. If you send a thank-you email within a few minutes or an hour of a meeting versus a few days or a week later, there's a significant difference in how people feel connected to it.

I encourage everyone to ask themselves: What type of digital body language am I projecting? How can I make sure I'm being clear and avoid being misunderstood in today's digital era?[38]

Erica Dhawan is the world's leading expert on digital body language and the author of Digital Body Language: How to Build Trust and Connection, No Matter the Distance.

9.4 The Secret to Better Virtual Communications

When I visit any group of students or am invited to do a guest lecture, I often share how lucky I feel that I was an English major as an undergraduate. The world has been moving toward English majors, I tell them, because many of our communications are based on being a good writer.

Great writing matters in everything from sending team emails to crafting a compelling online dating profile. Each day that passes, there seems to be yet another way that our personalities are defined by the things we choose to write and share online.

The secret to better communications is to become a better writer.

I realize that sounds intimidating, especially if you never thought of yourself as a writer or if you grew up hating to write. The good news is that, in my experience, becoming a better writer takes an unwavering focus on three principles:

1. **Write like you talk:** I spent many years studying screenwriting, and the one thing you learn from that is the rhythm of human dialogue. We can all use that to write in more human ways. There's a simple test to make sure you're doing this: Just read what you have written out loud. If it sounds like something you would in a conversation, keep it. If not, change it!

2. **Use just enough words:** Some people will tell you that less is more. To some degree, that's true. But there is such a thing with virtual communications as making it too short. A one-word email reply may seem like you're being clear, but it also can be misinterpreted. Instead of focusing on just brevity, focus on the combination of making it short and making it clear.

Don't use too many words, but don't use too few either.

3. **Always choose clarity:** Pontificating with lucid insights may demonstrate your enviable intellect. Simple words are usually better. I love vocabulary as much as the next English major, but the best communication has clarity. Be direct, choose your words intentionally, and say what you mean.

9.5 Three Tips for Better Emails When Working Remotely

You might be thinking this section is unnecessary. Do you really need a guide for better email? Perhaps you already have great habits when it comes to email, or maybe you could be a bit better. No matter what you think your level of savvy is, these tips are worth reviewing:

1. **Make the subject line relevant:** This line communicates the context, and sometimes it's the only thing people look at to decide whether they want to read the rest. Even if you're sending emails to colleagues that you know they will open, writing a great subject line can be as useful as being there in person to capture attention.

2. **Avoid writing "me-mails."** Email expert and author Gisela Hausmann cautions against starting all your emails with "I" or "my." Both put the focus on you instead of your reader. An alternative is to start with a phrase such as "Thank you." For example, instead of writing, "I wanted to follow up with you

on your concerns ...," you might say, "Thank you for raising your concerns ..."

3. **Start with what's most important**: A press release has a specific style. The most important information is in the first sentence, and every sentence that follows is less important. The assumption is that busy journalists won't read much, so public relations people know to put the most vital information up front. You should write your emails the same way.

9.6	**Three Tips for Using Instant or Team Messaging**

Nothing comes closer to the disruptive nature of just swinging by someone's office than instant messaging (IM). While its immediacy and ability to help people feel connected throughout the day are valuable, its potential to disrupt work is high. To use it well, consider these tips and share them with your colleagues:

1. **Set your availability:** Most IM tools come with a critical function: an availability indicator. You usually can set it to indicate that you are online/available or away/busy. This feature is there for a reason. If you use it consistently, and your colleagues do the same, it will work better for everyone.

2. **Direct your posts:** If you're using team messaging, make sure to indicate where your posts should go and who should see them.

This includes using category tags, segmenting your messages and tagging individuals if specific people need to see it. Though the ways you can do this may vary based on the tools you're using, the important thing is to add the necessary context to anything you share.

3. **Keep it light:** Instant messaging conversations are best for quick questions, easily addressed issues, or requests on things you already know. They are not good for longer, deeper conversations, or talks that include conflict or high emotion. Those are much better done in person and should be kept off IM.

9.7 How to Communicate in a Diverse Team

After spending five years working and living in Australia, I had become accustomed to the language of business down under. A few weeks after moving back to America, I realized I may need to rethink some of that language.

I remember sitting in a brainstorming meeting with colleagues and throwing out ideas. I used some profanity to illustrate a point and the look I saw on several people's faces immediately told me it was the wrong thing to say. Back in Sydney, this language was ordinary. Even tame.

A bit of profanity to indicate passion for an idea was no big deal in Australian work culture.

But now I was working in what was (and still is) one of the most politically correct cities in the world: Washington, D.C. People had different expectations, and I had to retrain myself when it came to my language.

I was lucky. That happened in person and I immediately saw the reaction from the team, corrected my language, and made a mental note to be more careful in the future. But what if that had been a virtual meeting? It's possible I may not have noticed the backlash, which is just one of the problems that can happen when people working remotely need to collaborate with those from different cultures.

> One of the fastest ways to appreciate and respect a culture is to notice and mirror their behaviors.

So how do you improve your intercultural intelligence? The first and most important lesson which I learned from my friend Paolo Nagari, a multicultural communications expert, is to fine-tune your powers of observation.

What language or gestures are the people on a call with you using?

How have they communicated with you over email or on the phone?

So, for example, if you are on a virtual call where they share how "honored" they are for you to be presenting, you reflect back that you are honored to be there as well. When you see that the team you're interacting with is highly hierarchical, make sure to address any questions to the person in charge and not to their subordinates.

Learning to respect another culture is a skill that you can develop with practice. What it requires most of all is constant observation and a willingness to integrate and immediately act on what you notice.

PERSPECTIVE:
LISETTE SUTHERLAND ON MULTICULTURAL ETIQUETTE

In some cultures, being direct is considered impolite. Or someone might equate accepting a compliment, even gracefully, as being conceited. Some see asking for feedback as a form of weakness. Some would be reluctant to pronounce an opinion before learning the views of those higher on the totem pole. Others refrain from making a decision before getting input from the entire group.

We can succeed in working with anyone, from anywhere, when we take the time to learn as much as we can about each other. Do what you can to learn about your remote colleagues' traditions and customs – including, ideally, the motivation and reasoning behind these customs.[39]

– *Lisette Sutherland is the author of* Work Together Anywhere.

CHAPTER SUMMARY
KEY TAKEAWAYS:

- To be a better virtual communicator, start with improving your writing: write like you talk, always choose clarity, and use just enough words (not too many and not too few).

- Your digital body language are the hidden cues in your digital communication that help people get to know you and what you really want.

- Better email communications start with avoiding "me mails," putting the focus on your reader instead and starting with what's most important.

- When working in a multicultural team, make sure you respect and consider the cultural differences.

CHAPTER 10

How to Build a Virtual Culture of Trust

A corporate culture comes from the beliefs of the leaders combined with the beliefs of the team. For many organizations, a corporate culture is based upon the office. In these buildings, teams spend eight hours a day, every day, collaborating, bonding, and working together side by side. This environment fosters teamwork because they are all literally in it together.

> Can you really create a work culture when people are dispersed and working remotely in locations all around the world?

Yes, but it is harder. In this chapter, we will look at some core principles of creating a virtual workplace culture of collaboration. We start with building the most important element that everything else is based upon: trust.

10.1	**Ten Rules for Building Trust in a Virtual Team**

My core team includes five colleagues all working remotely. I have worked with each of them for years. I have never met three of them in real life.

Though I do hope to make that happen sometime in the future, we have managed to build a trusted working relationship despite never having met in person. How did we do it?

By following ten key rules of building trust. Based on years of collaborating with virtual teams, these rules are the ones we have followed most faithfully. They will help you to foster a culture of trust among virtual teams as well.

VISIT ONLINE RESOURCES FOR:
A downloadable version of these rules for virtual trust.

1. **Start with empathy:** When colleagues are late, underperform, or miss a deadline, don't start by demanding an explanation or assume they aren't working hard. Instead, start by asking if everything is OK. Maybe they have a sick child at home, or they are overwhelmed with multiple assignments. Whatever the reason, always focus on the people first.

2. **Share information before they need it:** The most common way of sharing information is just in time. You send that email right before someone needs it. That feels like a job well done. The problem is that often sharing the information just in time is too late. Instead, involve people early and give them a chance to have input so they are more invested in the direction you are headed.

3. **Stand up for each other:** In an effective team, people stand up for each other. This is particularly true in a virtual team because it's too easy to assign blame or speak negatively about someone when you don't have to do it face to face.

4. **Give trust to get trust:** People trust those whom they believe trust them. It is a reciprocal effect that is hard-wired in most people. If you want to foster trust within a team as their leader, you need to start by trusting them.

5. **Set the tone:** How you interact with your team often sets the tone for everyone else. When you have a virtual meeting, what's the first thing you do? When you send a message, what language are you using? Lead by example, and others will follow.

6. **Be consistent:** Trustworthy people don't change their beliefs from week to week. They are constant and predictable in a good way when it matters.

7. **Do what you say you will do:** This is the definition of integrity, and it is also a sign of how trustworthy you are. Put simply,

people who act in this way earn our trust because they deserve it through their actions.

8. **Be available:** We are generally available to the most important people in our lives. They have our mobile numbers, and we answer immediately when they call. Can you do that for your closest teammates, too? Of course, it is important to set boundaries, but we need to know that if things go really bad, or if we have an urgent problem, our teammates and leaders will be there for us.

9. **Have a personality:** We trust people that we like, and we like people who are unafraid to be their authentic selves. It may be harder to do that in a virtual context, but the more you can find small ways to do it, the easier you make it for people to connect with you.

10. **Share the inside joke:** Within any virtual team, it can be easy for divisions to arise. Maybe the team members who are based closer together can bond over their shared love of a sports team that the others don't associate with. This type of bonding is common, and it's not a problem as long as it's not excluding people intentionally. Encourage teams to make it inclusive by inviting everyone to participate.

10.2 The Virtual "Signs" That Destroy Trust

We are generally good at making up our minds about how to trust someone based on signals that we see from behavior, but this changes in the virtual context. Since we can't always meet people face to face or rely on the usual nonverbal cues such as body language, we often make decisions about how to trust quickly based on the tiny signals we get through how they communicate with us.

In a world where these virtual signals are often all we have, it's a big deal to get them right and there is a serious impact when we get them wrong. Here are some of the biggest trust-killing behaviors that too many people engage in consistently – and that you should avoid:

1. **Refusing to get personal:** You know that video conference call where one person refuses to use video because the "webcam is broken"? We don't trust such people because they aren't willing to share themselves with us even though we are sharing with them.

2. **Enjoying your own tech illiteracy:** It is one thing to have a genuine struggle with technology, but there are people who seem to throw up their hands, declare themselves hopeless, and almost enjoy their tech ignorance. If the rest of us can figure

it out, you can, too. Or at least you can try harder and stress about it like a normal human.

3. **Giving bullshit excuses:** How many times have we had someone join a virtual meeting late and share an excuse that was clearly made up? Avoid this unnecessary bullshit. If you were late because you were changing a diaper while working from home, just be honest. It humanizes you and may end up making you more likeable as a result. As long as you're not always late, of course.

4. **Being unlikeable:** The main idea of my second book, called *Likeonomics*, was that people do business with people they like. So when you're rude, arrogant, or otherwise unlikeable, you make it hard for anyone to trust you or do business with you.

10.3 Team-Building Exercises That Work

One of the keys to growing a virtual team culture is to build trust through team building activities. The problem is that most of the team building we are used to doing happens in a physical way in the real world.

In a virtual setting, team building is critical, but it needs to go beyond asking everyone to answer an interesting question at the start of your next virtual meeting.

Andrew Long, founder of collaboration platform Connectify, says that "managers should seek remote team activities that support mental wellness, connect team members on a more personal level, and normalize working from home."[40]

What types of exercises could work to do this? Improv coach and corporate trainer Jessie Shternshus has one suggestion for how to help teams bond when collaborating virtually. Here's how it works:

"A facilitator introduces him/herself to the group and includes four or five interesting personal facts. Everybody in the group then introduces themselves, tying a fact about themselves back to a fact from the facilitator's intro. Just ONE of the facts you share needs to tie back. You can tie back to ANY of the participants that already introduced themselves. Keep going until everyone is introduced."[41]

10.4	**How to Break Down Silos**

Contributed by Jamie Notter and Maddie Grant, authors of **The Non-Obvious Guide to Employee Engagement.**

Workplace culture is one of the few remaining areas where organizations differentiate themselves from competitors, but it works only when you get past the branding communications part of culture work and start treating it with the same seriousness you give to finances and other core management functions.

To set the record straight, organizational silos are not necessarily a problem. It makes sense to have people who share deep expertise in a particular domain to work closely together.

> Sometimes staying in your swim lane can make everyone faster.

Where silos betray us, however, is when the strength of our boundaries and territories prevents adequate information exchange or proactive problem solving that requires multiple perspectives.

In an office environment, we can literally walk down the hall to make our boundaries more porous, but as work becomes more virtual, you need to develop some additional strategies. Here are three concrete suggestions.

TIP 1 MEET TO "CONNECT THE DOTS"

You should convene a cross-functional team via video periodically, but don't just go around and report what you're working on. Task participants to show up with specific areas of overlap, coordination, or collaboration that's needed. You don't need to solve everything at the meeting; the right people can connect after to do that.

TIP 2 CREATE A "TCB" CHANNEL

That stands for "taking care of business," and I've used it within a remote team as a channel where everyone provides a daily one-sentence report on what they worked on. This is not about showing accountability or proving that you're busy; it's to create visibility into how the whole system is operating so problems or opportunities can be identified proactively.

TIP 3 USE IDEA MANAGEMENT SOFTWARE

Programs such as IdeaScale let anyone in your organization suggest ideas or innovations. Then everyone else votes them up or down, and the ones with the most up-votes get considered for action. This solution is designed to accelerate innovation, but it also adds visibility across silos as to who is suggesting or voting for different ideas. Managers can scan the activity through that lens and start to make connections for possible collaboration earlier on.

Notice that the purpose of these silo-busting activities is never just to bust the silos. It's to solve problems, identify opportunities, improve collaboration, increase speed, and eliminate redundancy. A strong remote working culture should always be about making your people more successful.

VISIT ONLINE RESOURCES FOR:
An excerpt from *The Non-Obvious Guide to Employee Engagement.*

Jamie Notter and Maddie Grant are the co-founders of Human Workplaces and the authors of several books on workplace culture, including **When Millennials Take Over** *and the* **Non-Obvious Guide to Employee Engagement.**

CHAPTER SUMMARY
KEY TAKEAWAYS:

- Trust is the foundation for a strong virtual team culture and is built on a foundation of empathy.

- To build trust with virtual teammates, you must be consistent, give trust to get it, be available, and do what you say you will do.

- Beware of the warning signs that someone is not trustworthy, such as refusing to get personal, giving bullshit excuses, or making themselves unlikeable.

- To break down silos in a team, meet to connect the dots and use digital tools to improve transparent communications.

CHAPTER 11

How to Lead a Remote Team

When I think back to the many bosses I had before I became an entrepreneur, I not so fondly remember one as the worst. She had a habit of joining a project that was nearly complete and making a decision that would force everyone to start over.

We blamed her inability to understand our work on her failing to be there with us. It took me years to realize that her working remotely wasn't the biggest problem. The real issue was her lack of leadership skills.

> Leadership flaws can become more destructive when leading a virtual team, but are rarely caused by the remote work itself.

Leading a team effectively while working remotely does require a different way of thinking and a different style of connecting. Let's consider what's most important in leadership for a remote team.

11.1 Five Tips for Leading a Remote Team

Leading a team in one or more locations doesn't mean you have to rethink the practice of leadership.

Good leaders care about their people. They make clear what they expect and inspire people to work toward a larger goal. These qualities are important when leading a remote team as well.

Beyond basic leadership principles, there are some specific practices that will help you to lead a remote team better.

TIP 1 DROP IN HELPFULLY

A management principle from the 1980s promotes the idea of "managing by walking around." Obviously, that's not possible when you have a remote team, but you can find ways to drop in unexpectedly via phone calls, instant messaging, or email. The key is to do it without resorting to micromanaging or making your team members feel distrusted. Instead, keep your tone positive, ask if they need anything, and offer to help.

PERSPECTIVE:
KEVIN EIKENBERRY ON CHECKING IN

I have a personal goal of checking in with at least three of my team members each day and with everyone at least once a week. If you and your team are new to remote, I would make that more frequent. While you can use instant messages and email, pick up the phone or fire up your webcam for more of these check-ins.[42]

– *Kevin Eikenberry is the co-author of* The Long-Distance Leader *with Wayne Turmel.*

TIP 2 MAKE MEETINGS DUAL PURPOSE

In the real world, meetings often are seen as matter-of-fact gatherings. We walk with strict agendas and redirect any conversation that seems off-topic. When doing virtual meetings, as we learned in Part 2, it is equally important to have direction and keep people on task. However, these meetings have another important purpose that leaders need to remember.

Virtual meetings may be the only opportunities for human connection a remote team member gets with colleagues.

When you have a team working remotely, the virtual meeting can serve the emotional need for connection among team members as well. It is important not to dismiss this opportunity for connection and bonding in the name of efficiency.

TIP 3 OFFER CONSISTENT INSPIRATION

What could you do that would become your trademark within your team? Some of the best remote leaders I have interviewed became experts at creating traditions and expectations among their team by consistently doing something that engaged them as people.

TIP 4 CREATE SYNCHRONOUS MOMENTS

What if you could create moments of synchronicity where the team gathered at the same time every day or every week for inspiration? When something big happened, what if you created a moment of celebration virtually? A remote team can share these bonding times, but they need to be intentionally planned and executed.

If a meeting is quickly started and finished, or if remote workers don't have a chance to contribute, then they may end up feeling disconnected. Does this mean you should stretch every meeting out? Probably not.

Remember that your meetings and other moments when you bring a team together are not only times to get work done. They also offer important opportunities for bonding and conversations. As a leader, it's your job to support this human need.

TIP 5 ALWAYS HAVE A "BECAUSE"

The first step to getting buy-in and having teams be accountable is ensuring they know why they are doing something. This becomes even more important when you are leading a remote team because the dependencies between what people are doing can become hard to see.

> Everyone works better when they know *why* they need to do something.

For example, in my publishing business, I might have a website designer working on a new series of templates and a programmer waiting on the final design in order to make the site. If that designer doesn't know her deadline is tight because the programmer needs enough time to do the site, she misses the context of why she was asked to work more quickly than usual.

11.2	How to Fix Common Problems with Remote Teams

Perhaps the biggest danger with remote work is the lack of visibility into what we, our colleagues, and our teams are doing.

> Without transparency, people invent stories to explain what they perceive to be happening.

The only way to combat this effect is to find new ways to make the invisible more visible. Here are some ways to do it.

TIP 1 OFFER PROACTIVE UPDATES

Start by keeping team members updated proactively. This might be through a daily email update of tasks completed and jobs that are still in progress. You might use a project management tool or time-tracking software. Regardless of the method, the more transparency you and your team can introduce with others, the more connected everyone will feel.

TIP 2 SHOW YOUR WORK

When I am writing a book, a big part of the process is doing all the research and interviews beforehand. This work is extensive, but it can be easy to discount or miss. I typically take photos of the process and share them with my audience throughout as I'm writing. Here's an example with index cards I used to map the story flow for the book you're reading now.

By sharing these images while writing, I could engage more people in the process and offer an inside look at the effort involved. As a result, when people eventually read the book, they had a foundation to build on.

TIP 3 BROADCAST YOUR ABSENCE

The proverb that "absence makes the heart grow fonder" usually refers to matters of love, but it relates to remote teams as well. When you will be away from your desk, consider making that apparent through out-of-office responders, away-status settings, or instant messaging tools. Not only will colleagues realize when you're not working, but also you can remind everyone of when you are there and working.

TIP 4 MAKE PUBLIC COMMITMENTS

If you can do the opposite and make a public commitment for when you will complete a task, you will stand out. The people who proactively choose to be accountable before being asked are the ones who we tend to trust the most.

> We have all worked with people who avoid committing to anything. No one trusts those people.

This can also be accomplished by using software. Project management and collaboration platform Asana refers to this as a "central source of truth." As Asana Head of Global Community Joshua Zerkel says, "part of what makes remote work work and work well is if you're really clear on what it is you and your team are doing."[43]

PERSPECTIVE:
HARRY MOSELEY ON MEASURING PRODUCTIVITY

Measuring productivity for remote employees should be the same as measuring productivity in the office. You don't watch each person to make sure they are programming or writing emails or taking calls in the office. They have deliverables, and if they don't deliver on them, then you know they aren't working.[44]

– Harry Moseley is the Global CIO for the meeting platform Zoom.

TIP 5 DON'T STAY ON MUTE

Going on mute is polite in a virtual meeting, but if you stay silent for every meeting, then you take the risk that your teammates will forget you're there. Depending on the meeting format, you can participate by sharing your point of view in conversation or by contributing to the chat. Either way, the important thing is to find a way to participate and have something valuable to say when you do.

11.3	**How to Improve Accountability**

Contributed by Jonathan Raymond, founder of Refound and author of Good Authority.

Imagine you need to have an accountability conversation with someone who is not in a good place. The person is on edge and more likely to be defensive or secretive about what's going on. Instead, you need demonstrable change quickly.

How do you negotiate this tight spot? Here's a three-step process to engage with this person and turn things for the better:

1. **Show care even if you may not want to.** Start with curiosity. Ask how the person is doing and seek to understand. Try to accept, as hard as it may be, that this is something you probably should have coached the person on long before this moment.

2. **Stoke curiosity even though you feel like you shouldn't have to.** Ask the person for perspective on whatever you're seeing. Follow up with questions about other options or approaches the person can come up with that might be better. Listen and consider the merits.

3. **Be courageous even if things might get worse.** Be honest about your concern. Be clear about what you do and don't need. Protecting someone from the truth only prolongs guessing about where the person stands and what you need. Hint: Step 3 is likely to backfire if you skip steps 1 and 2.[45]

11.4	How to Manage Conflict in a Remote Team

Conflict is inevitable in any team, but when it happens in a remote work group, it can escalate to become much worse.

This is not necessarily a function of time. Yes, conflict with remote work can build up as people keep frustrations bottled up. It also can blow up over an insensitive email or perceived slight through digital communications.

Most advice you find about resolving workplace conflict starts with a single suggestion: Do it face to face. What if that isn't possible?

When a conflict arises between remote work teammates, it is still a good idea to get people together, ideally on video, to address the issue.

> To manage a conflict, start with understanding and managing the most common responses people have to the conflict.

To help you do that, here are the most common responses to conflict we commonly see with remote teams and how to handle each one.

RESPONSE 1 GHOSTING/SILENCE

When dealing with conflict, some people just shut down and stop communicating. They may start by "ghosting" (ignoring) the team member they have a conflict with, and this could extend to them becoming more withdrawn and less engaged overall. The best way to deal with this response is to get them talking about what's causing the issue, so you can address it.

RESPONSE 2 RETRIBUTION/SABOTAGE

Some people who feel wronged decide that they will find their own way to even the score through workplace vengeance or sabotage. If you see this happening, the best way to prevent it is to show the vengeful person the human and business costs of such actions. If you can convey how their behavior might hinder the team or harm their own interests, you may be able to get them to rethink their behavior.

RESPONSE 3 AGGRESSION/ANGER

In a conflict, some people respond with aggression immediately or after the situation escalates. They lash out and act with emotion first. When you're dealing with this, the first thing to do is move the conflict away from virtual communications tools. Anger expressed through emails or instant messages can be much more damaging because it's impossible to take back. Instead, try to move the dialogue to a more human place with live interaction so you can help those involved address it constructively.

PERSPECTIVE:
JAMIE NOTTER ON ADDRESSING CONFLICTS IMMEDIATELY

It sounds simple but make a habit of moving toward the conflict when it emerges. Most people choose to wait – for more information, or a better time, or after you can get some advice – but this delay almost always allows the conflict to grow and become more complex. Instead, the moment you get an email that rubs you the wrong way or hear a comment in the video meeting that seems off base, have the conversation about it as soon as you can. When conflicts are new, they are much easier to resolve.

– *Jamie Notter is co-author of* The Non-Obvious Guide To
  Employee Engagement.

Despite applying these techniques, you may not be able to resolve the conflict through virtual means, and then you have only two alternatives. Either you get everyone together physically and address the conflict face to face, or you take concrete steps to transfer team members or let someone go if it's serious enough.

11.5 Emotional Intelligence in a Virtual Setting

Contributed by Kerry Goyette, author of **The Non-Obvious Guide to Emotional Intelligence.**

Often, people think emotional intelligence (EQ) is only about me. They think all they have to do is be more self-aware and more empathetic, and boom: EQ boost.

But that's not the whole picture.

EQ is the intelligent use of emotion to make better decisions and adapt more effectively to your environment. High EQ means you go beyond me and into we and why. It means you account for the system surrounding the individual. When it comes to conflict, which I call people problem solving, a high EQ response can make you a Jedi of problem solving.

Here's what you need to know for navigating conflict the EQ way:

→ Know what sets you off. What causes an emotional response in which you avoid a conflict or win at all costs? Know your triggers and the meaning you've attached to them.

→ Do some perspective-taking. High EQ means looking at the different sides of a conflict. Most people don't show up to work thinking about how they can ruin your day. People have reasons for their positions. Seek to understand and consider them.

→ People with high EQ move beyond seeing conflict as simply win-lose. They aim to problem-solve or compromise.

→ Brainstorm alternatives that can solve the problem. Ask others how they've solved similar problems.

→ Discuss options on how both parties can win. Is a compromise possible?

→ Look for ways to help and support others at work. Helping is not just about the other person; it gives you a social boost as well.

Bonus: People who help others typically receive higher performance ratings.

VISIT ONLINE RESOURCES FOR:
An excerpt from *The Non-Obvious Guide to Emotional Intelligence.*

EQ means understanding your environment. In virtual settings, it's easier to feel stress or fear because it's harder to connect informally. There's no drop-in or chitchat unless we make it happen. And the latest neuroscience research shows that our brains require social connection to thrive.

The company of others helps us regulate our own emotions, makes tasks feel easier, and puts our fears in perspective. In a virtual world, all connection has to become intentional.

EQ is not extra. It's essential. To be human is to be connected.

Kerry Goyette is the founder and president of Aperio Consulting Group and a certified behavior analyst.

CHAPTER SUMMARY
KEY TAKEAWAYS:

- Effective remote team leaders drop in helpfully, offer consistent inspiration, and always share the "because" behind the work.

- The biggest cause of remote team conflicts is a lack of transparency. Offer proactive updates and show your work to help prevent conflict.

- To improve team accountability, show care even when you may not want to and be honest as well as clear about what you do and don't need.

CHAPTER 12

Hiring and Building a Future-Proof Team

One thing you can count on disruptive events to do is expose problems that already exist. If a team had difficulty collaborating or gravitated toward complacency, those tendencies will worsen in a crisis.

In the immediate aftermath of the COVID-19 pandemic, the companies that already had moved toward allowing teams to work remotely and had systems up and running to enable virtual collaboration were quickest to adjust. Over time, they probably will rebound the fastest.

What does it take to build a team like that or to succeed while working in one? In this chapter, we will look at some critical aspects of building a diverse and inclusive team that can adapt to the world and maintain its flexibility as a competitive advantage.

12.1 What Most Teams Forget About Real Diversity

For the past several years, diversity and inclusion have become hot topics in business – and for good reason. There are even growing reports that diverse workplaces are more financially successful.[46] But what is diversity?

> Diversity is being invited to the party; inclusion is being asked to dance.

This frequently shared quote from consultant and cultural innovator Vernā Myer[47] is perhaps even more true when it comes to finding ways to engage a team that is distributed remotely.

The problem with diversity, though, is that it is usually seen through a single dimension: demographics. So if you have a team with a mix of genders, ages, abilities, and cultural backgrounds, then you have diversity, right?

Unfortunately, that leaves out a second important element: a diversity of experience. Do you have someone on the team who comes from a different industry background? Is anyone in the group accustomed to living in a rural setting rather than an urban area? Is there a mix of extroverts and introverts and a variety of preferred working styles?

> A team that is truly diverse will often need to work harder to understand one another. That is a good thing.

A team with members who put in the daily effort to better empathize with one another is a team that will be able to do the same thing with customers.

12.2 Three Secrets of Hiring Amazing Remote Workers

There are dozens of books devoted to people who are seeking a remote working lifestyle. Some promise that you can live your dream by working from the beach. Others promise flexibility that may be required due to family situations.

What should you look for if you're considering bringing on team members to work remotely? Conversely, if you're looking for a new role that would allow you to work remotely, how you might position yourself? Here are three secrets that will help you to hire the best possible remote team member.

SECRET 1 PRIORITIZE PROACTIVITY

When you're working with people you don't see every day, it is critical that they are self-starters. Look for signs of this early. Have they done their homework, and are they asking relevant questions? Do they follow up when they say they will? These behaviors are key indicators that someone may have the right mindset to be a valuable contributor to the team.

SECRET 2 SEEK DIVERSITY

Beyond looking for diverse team members of different genders and ethnicities, you should consider whether the people you are considering see your industry or your business differently than you. Are you interviewing neurodiverse candidates or welcome those with disabilities? What about people over 50? Real diversity requires you to create an inclusive environment that welcomes people of all abilities and backgrounds.

SECRET 3 FORGIVE THE "GAP YEARS"

When people start a business, take a break from work to travel, or decide to become a parent, they end up with a gap in their experience. Those gaps are sometimes a few months, sometimes a few years. Either way, part of the reason people seek remote work is to balance the various aspects of their life.

Rather than focus on why someone was not working in a traditional role for a specific period, ask what they learned during those gap years and whether they have the right experience to make a valuable contribution to the team.

| 12.3 | **How to Ace the Virtual Interview (Whether You're the Interviewer or the Interviewee)** |

A clip from the 2013 film *The Internship* shows two sales guys (played by Vince Vaughn and Owen Wilson) trying to land an internship at Google, despite their age and lack of tech ability.They do a virtual interview over a webcam from a public library and seem to be failing hilariously, but then they land the internship.

It turns out they managed to do what's often the hardest thing in their virtual interview: demonstrate a personality. If you're being interviewed virtually or if you're on the other side conducting the interview, one often forgotten priority should similarly be to find ways to be more authentic.

How do you discover the personality of the interview subject or demonstrate your personality in a virtual setting? Here are a few tips:

→ **Make sure technology isn't a barrier.** Practice with the tools and become comfortable using them before the interview so your conversation can be as natural as possible.

→ **Choose the right background.** What can you include behind you that offers a little insight about you or your organization? Make it appropriately personal, and you can offer the right cues to guide the conversation.

→ **Do your homework.** When you're interviewing someone, make sure you have gone through the person's credentials so you can ask insightful questions. If you're being interviewed, do your research on the organization so you have a point of view to share and questions to ask that show your thinking process.

→ **Integrate props.** Sometimes the best way to show what you mean or what you've done is to grab something physical to share. This could be a book you're reading or a project you recently completed. Panning the camera around the office will show your surroundings.

12.4 How to Conduct a Virtual Onboarding Program

Contributed by Greg Besner, author of The Culture Quotient.

As the trend for employees to work remotely continues to accelerate, onboarding new hires in a virtual environment will also become customary. Companies will want to be even more proactive to ensure that remote workers assimilate and complement their ideal company culture. Here are a few best practices for virtually onboarding employees and putting your company culture front and center:

→ **Video Onboarding.** Use video conferencing to introduce your new employees to as many employees as possible. Using video conferencing will allow new employees to interact with team members in many roles and locations, and to see and hear your culture in action.

→ **Assign Mentors.** Connect your new employees with experienced employees to mentor them during this critical onboarding period. Make sure the mentors are strong representatives of your ideal company culture and core values.

→ **Virtual Company Tours.** If you have some office videos and photo archives that highlight your company culture, you can compile this information to share as a virtual tour. This can be another opportunity to celebrate your culture.

→ **Be Creative.** There is no limit to creative ideas to remotely onboard new employees. Be thoughtful, proactive, and authentic, and your new employees will be excited to help foster your ideal culture.

Greg Besner is the founder and Vice Chairman of CultureIQ and the author of The Culture Quotient.

12.5	**Five Trends Changing the Future of Work**

If you are a reader of my Non-Obvious Trend series, you know that I have spent much of the past decade thinking and writing about trends. Most of this work has focused on trends and shifts in business and consumer behavior. Many of the trends are useful to describe a shift in how we work as well.

VISIT ONLINE RESOURCES FOR:
An excerpt featuring trends *Non-Obvious Megatrends*.

As a spotlight, here are five trends that describe this shift and are worth considering as you think about building a future-proof team for your organization or becoming a team member.

1. **Amplified Identity:** As individualism rises globally, people are carefully cultivating how they are perceived, chasing stardom, and making themselves vulnerable to criticism in the process. This relates to the importance of your personal brand to your identity, as discussed in Chapter 4.

2. **Instant Knowledge:** As we consume bite-sized bits of knowledge on demand, we benefit from learning everything more quickly but risk forgetting the value of mastery and wisdom. One result of this megatrend is that

a wider range of learning content is being produced and consumed through virtual channels, making the creation and consumption of webinars and online learning that we explored in Chapter 8 increasingly important.

3. **Revivalism:** Overwhelmed by new technology and the complexity of life, people seek out simpler experiences that offer nostalgia and remind them of a more trustworthy time. We will continue to see manifestations of this megatrend in how we create effective remote working spaces (which we reviewed in Chapter 3) and how we embrace the remote working lifestyle (as covered in Chapter 2).

4. **Human Mode:** Tired of technology that isolates us from one another, people seek out and place greater value on physical, authentic, and "unperfect" experiences. The human connection will continue to be critical. Bringing this humanity to virtual conversations (or presentations) and how to build trusted relationships while working remotely were extensively covered in Chapters 6, 7, 9, and 10.

5. **Flux Commerce:** The lines between industries erode, leading to a continual disruption of business models, distribution channels, and consumer expectations. This shifting nature of business and the type of mindset required to embrace this near-constant change were topics we considered in Chapter 2 and this chapter.

Non-Obvious Megatrends, *the tenth and final installment in the* Non-Obvious *series, was a #1* Wall Street Journal *bestseller and has been read or shared by more than a million readers.*

CHAPTER SUMMARY
KEY TAKEAWAYS:

- Diversity means more than simply having team members from different backgrounds. It also means having teammates with different perspectives who can challenge one another.

- When hiring remote team members, prioritize candidates who are proactive, seek a diversity of opinions, and be ready to forgive "gap years."

- In a virtual interview, make sure technology isn't a barrier to relaying your true personality and do your homework to offer a valuable perspective.

Surviving the Future of Work

This book has been a labor of love and necessity. We live in a world where everyone needs to be fluent in how to work remotely and run or participate in virtual meetings.

But teaching people these skills is not what I usually do.

> My mission is to help people see what others miss.

That's what I have spoken about to hundreds of thousands of people over the past few years. It's also what I have been doing for the past decade by researching trends and teaching executives my methods for becoming a non-obvious thinker.

I have often written that I believe that trends are simply curated observations of the accelerating present. And our present is certainly accelerating.

Since the COVID-19 pandemic, everyone wants to know what to expect for the future. In a time of uncertainty, we need help to make sense of everything.

After a decade of studying patterns to isolate and identify emerging trends – there is one principle that has helped me to stay flexible enough to adapt when changes come ... no matter how disruptive they are:

| Always be curious.

I have become a collector of what sometimes seems like useless knowledge. It has become my secret to success.

The first time I heard about the emerging field of cloud seeding – the science of controlling the rain – I spent an entire afternoon reading about it. To prepare for a talk last year, I attended a 90-minute seminar on how to sell a diamond engagement ring.

The more narrowly you define your expertise or your beliefs, the harder it is to adapt when confronted by serious change.

And serious change is already here. In fact, it is likely that the way you are working right now will be vastly different ten years from now. For some people, that is a terrifying thought. For others, it's exciting. I'm choosing to be excited.

I hope you do too.

Reading List

While gathering insights for this book, I downloaded or purchased dozens of books on the topics of virtual leadership and teams, remote work, virtual collaboration, and many other related topics.

These are some of the books that I highly recommend for further reading:

1. **Work Together Anywhere: A Handbook on Working Remotely** by Lisette Sutherland and Kirsten Janene-Nelson

2. **The Long-Distance Leader: Rules for Remarkable Remote Leadership** by Kevin Eikenberry

3. **Remote: Office Not Required** by Jason Fried and David Heinemeier Hansson

4. **Influencing Virtual Teams: 17 Tactics That Get Things Done with Your Remote Employees** by Hassan Osman

5. **The Definitive Guide to Facilitating Remote Workshops** by Mark Tippen, Jim Kalbach, and David Chin

Glossary of Terms

→ **Asynchronous communication** – any type of communication that does not happen in real time where there is some time lag between messages (i.e., email).

→ **Attention residue** – a term based on the work of researcher Sophie Leroy, this is when thoughts about a task persist and intrude while performing another task.

→ **Backchannel** – when technology is used to have a real-time conversation alongside another event (live or virtual) happening at the same time.

→ **Co-working office** – a working space that provides essentials for work such as WiFi and meeting space that is shared by workers who usually do not work at the same company.

→ **Deep work** – a term originally coined by author Cal Newport to describe activities performed in a high-concentration environment free from any type of distraction.

→ **Design Sprint** – a process used mainly by small technical teams to develop and build a prototype for an idea in a matter of days.

→ **Digital body language** – a term used alternately to describe the subtext of digital conversations as well as the specific signals that can be seen by watching how people behave when using digital tools.

→ **Digital nomad** – an individual who uses technology to enable a working lifestyle where they can travel the world and live anywhere.

→ **Digital whiteboard** – an open collaborative space online that works like a whiteboard in real life, allowing multiple people to share ideas in real time in a single location.

→ **Hot desks** – an office format where individual workspaces are openly assigned on a rotating basis, often as a cost-saving method.

→ **Hybrid work** – a combination of working remotely and coming into a physical office.

→ **Hybrid event** – a gathering that has a live component along with participants who use technology to participate virtually.

→ **Reverse mentoring** – a workplace arrangement that pairs younger employees with executive team members to mentor them on various topics of strategic and cultural relevance.

→ **Shallow work** – a term coined by author Cal Newport to describe activities done often through multitasking that don't require significant concentration.

→ **Sizzle reel** – a short, often flashy video used to promote a product or service.

→ **Synchronous communication** – any communication that happens in real time (i.e., talking on the phone, in-person conversations)

→ **Telecommuting** – the original term used for working out of the office, usually from home without the need for commuting. Often used as a synonym for working from home (WFH) or remote work.

→ **Virtual background** – a feature in some video conference software platforms that allows you to display an image or video as your background virtually.

Endnotes

1. Pg 13 – *Remote: Office Not Required* by Jason Fried and David Heinemeier Hansson
2. https://www.owllabs.com/state-of-remote-work/2018
3. https://www.citylab.com/life/2015/12/the-invention-of-telecommuting/418047/
4. https://www.owllabs.com/state-of-remote-work/2018
5. https://www.menshealth.com/sex-women/a19524626/why-long-commutes-lead-to-divorce/
6. https://globalworkplaceanalytics.com/resources/costs-benefits
7. https://youtu.be/oiUyyZPIHyY
8. https://www.inc.com/brit-morse/remote-work-survey-owl-labs.html
9. https://hbr.org/podcast/2020/03/adjusting-to-remote-work-during-the-coronavirus-crisis
10. Pg 1 – *Silent Messages* by Albert Mehrabian.
11. https://youtu.be/oiUyyZPIHyY
12. https://www.shellypalmer.com/2020/03/desk-jockey-badass-remote-worker-easy-steps/
13. https://austinkleon.com/2020/03/11/a-working-from-home-manual-in-disguise/
14. https://stories.buffer.com/my-morning-routine-as-a-remote-ceo-and-why-its-always-changing-14773c4a95b3
15. https://www.brianfanzo.com/forced-to-work-from-home-with-adhd-now-what/
16. https://melrobbins.com/blog/five-elements-5-second-rule/
17. From an email interview with Pamela Slim.
18. From an email interview with Neen James.
19. https://medium.com/@tacaponi_7153/the-sales-sales-leadership-loneliness-epidemic-7bf15690be6e
20. Pg. 3 – *Deep Work* by Cal Newport

21. https://ideas.repec.org/a/eee/jobhdp/v109y2009i2p168-181.html
22. From an email interview with Mitch Joel.
23. https://brandmanagecamp.com/blog/7-zoom-video-mistakes/
24. From an email interview with Brie Reynolds.
25. From an email interview with Henry Mason.
26. https://www.nytimes.com/2020/04/14/us/zoom-meetings-gender.html
27. From an email interview with Greg Roth.
28. https://youtu.be/vYwN2LFDeFA
29. https://lauragassnerotting.com/2020/03/30/trust/
30. Pg 22 – *Steal the Show* by Michael Port
31. https://www.linkedin.com/pulse/why-we-must-avoid-superficial-content-carmen-simon/
32. https://blog.webex.com/video-conferencing/why-screen-sharing-works-better-for-sales-than-traditional-conference-calls/
33. https://www.linkedin.com/pulse/advanced-speakers-avoid-apologies-carmen-simon/
34. https://www.jaybaer.com/7-virtual-event-success-factors/
35. https://www.psfk.com/2020/03/virtual-events-live-streaming.html
36. https://youtu.be/HDxVHY8d6-g
37. https://youtu.be/E82atOgbfJ4
38. https://www.marshallgoldsmith.com/articles/hows-your-digital-body-language/
39. Pg 218 – *Working Together Anywhere* by Lisette Sutherland
40. From an email interview with Andrew Long.
41. From an email interview with Jessie Shternshus.
42. https://blog.kevineikenberry.com/leadership-supervisory-skills/five-things-leaders-of-newly-remote-teams-must-do/
43. https://blog.asana.com/2020/03/asana-tips-work-from-anywhere/
44. https://blog.zoom.us/wordpress/2020/04/06/cio-panel-best-practices-for-enabling-remote-workforce/
45. https://refound.com/2020/03/26/in-a-crisis-dont-confuse-loud-with-worse/
46. https://www.thebalance.com/cultural-diversity-3306201
47. https://www.refinery29.com/en-us/2017/05/156009/harvard-business-school-diversity-issue-essay

Index

About the Author

Rohit Bhargava is on a mission to help the world be more open-minded by teaching others how to be non-obvious thinkers. He is the founder of the Non-Obvious Company and an entertaining, original, and "non-boring" keynote speaker on innovation and trust. He previously spent 15 years in leadership roles at two renowned ad agencies: Leo Burnett and Ogilvy. Rohit is the #1 *Wall Street Journal* bestselling author of 7 books and has been invited to deliver keynote presentations in 32 countries around the world. His insights have been used by the World Bank, NASA, Intel, Disney, Colgate Swissotel, Coca-Cola, Schwab, Under Armour, NBC Universal, American Express, and hundreds of others to win the future. Rohit is a popular Adjunct Professor of Marketing and Storytelling at Georgetown University and also writes a monthly column for *GQ* magazine in Brazil. He believes in listening before talking, is a lifelong lover of the Olympics, actively hates cauliflower, and lives and works with his wife and two boys in the Washington, D.C., area.

Get new ideas to help you win the future!

JOIN MY FREE EMAIL NEWSLETTER:

www.rohitbhargava.com/subscribe

Every week you will get a curated email featuring the most interesting and underappreciated stories of the week – along with short insights on what they mean for you.